EINSTEIN DISCOVERED TH[...] WHILE DOZING. WHAT CREATIVE BREAKTHROUGHS CAN YOUR UNCONSCIOUS MAKE?

Researchers know that under the right conditions our unconscious can make extraordinary breakthroughs. This book is designed to break down those barriers around your unconscious mind and ignite your inner creative forces with 28 specific, powerful exercises. From understanding how your creativity can be stifled to heightening your dream states, this book shows how to:

- Discover your true direction in life and follow it
- Use your creative unconscious to boost your self-esteem
- Become more flexible and self-aware in your personal and professional life
- Overcome creative blocks
- Deal with difficult personal problems by making them into dreams—and resolving the problem through dreamwork.

"*Creative Breakthroughs* shows people how to tap their creativity through exercises that take them off-guard and allow them to circumvent their habitual resistances. I recommend this book for anyone who wishes to free his or her creative energy and break through creative blocks."
> —LESLIE ROSENTHAL, Ph.D.,
> Dean of Group Psychotherapy Studies,
> Center for Modern Psychoanalytic Studies,
> author of *Resolving Resistance in Group Psychotherapy*

"*Creative Breakthroughs* is sharp and focused . . . and sure to help anyone interested in finding out more about themselves and fulfilling their creative potential. The exercises are practical and challenging."
> —ROBERT WELBER,
> founder of Studio Elementary School, Manhattan,
> certified psychoanalyst

CREATIVE
BREAKTHROUGHS

Tap the Power of Your Unconscious Mind

JILL MORRIS, PH.D.

WARNER BOOKS

A Time Warner Company

Warner Books, Inc., 1271 Avenue of the Americas, New York, NY 10020

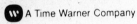 A Time Warner Company

Printed in the United States of America
First printing: March 1992
10 9 8 7 6 5 4 3 2 1

Library of Congress Cataloging-in-Publication Data

Morris, Jill (Jill Carlotta)
    Creative breakthroughs : tap the power of your unconscious mind / by Jill Morris.
        p.   cm.
    Includes bibliographical references.
    ISBN 0-446-39217-0
    1. Creative ability.   2. Creative thinking.   3. Inspiration.
I. Title.
BF408.M625   1992
153.3'5—dc20   91-7201
                                                                  CIP

Book design by Giorgetta Bell McRee
Cover design and illustration by Anne Twomey

Dedication

My gratitude to all those students, patients, and friends who contributed their valued experiences to this book.

And to those special teachers who have guided me through the exhilarating and terrible journey of change and creative growth.

And especially to my mother—whose originality and sense of wonderment—gave me the impetus to embark upon a path that she, sadly, lacked the encouragement and conviction to pursue.

Contents

CONTENTS

PART ONE

Preparation

1

INTRODUCTION: THE FOUR STEPS TO CREATIVITY

Could a creative break-through change your life? Imagine proposing a brilliant idea at a board meeting and winning the contract. Or creating one fabulous meal after another from your own original recipes. Planting a dazzling display of flowers according to your own sense of design. Getting in touch with the deep mysterious part of yourself through painting. Creativity is about affirming your life—not just making masterpieces. It's about filling your life with wonder and excitement, enjoying and growing in relationships, getting more satisfaction out of your job and hobbies. It's about doing whatever you do better than before. And it's even about doing the so-called impossible, because you're able to see the old problem in a new light. Creativity is the spark of originality, of inspiration, of illumination that mixes fresh colors, invents new products, arrives at ground-breaking solutions.

Creativity, according to most artists, psychologists, and scholars, originates in the unconscious. In periods when we are conscientiously and deeply engaged in a task or problem, if we temporarily stop working, our unconscious minds continue to work on that same task or problem, expanding and elaborating upon it, while we are at rest. It is during these moments that a creative breakthrough can take place. It is no miracle that Einstein's theory of relativity came to him while he was dozing, that Descartes conceived his rationalistic theory upon which all 18th-century thinking was based during a dream, or that Beethoven composed a canon in his sleep. And on the less lofty scale, golf pro Jack Nicklaus discovered in a dream a new golf grip that made the winning difference in his game. And it doesn't only happen when we are dreaming. Creative breakthroughs can also occur during waking moments when our conscious minds are distracted—while we are brushing our teeth or mowing the lawn.

The creative process that accounts for these inspirations was first described by Aristotle in *Metaphysics* and in our time has been elaborated upon by John Dewey, Rollo May, and Graham Wallas. There are four basic stages of the creative process that can lead to breakthroughs. First is the *preparation* stage: collecting, searching, reading, thinking, and letting your mind wander. Next follows *incubation*, the stage at which your unconscious reorganizes and elaborates on the collected material. The third stage is *illumination*, when you are able to see the solution in an experience, an intuition, an insight, a hunch or a feeling of rightness. And last is *verification*—the furnishing of the necessary proof or evaluation of the solution.

Inspiration plays a major role in this process. In the

past, when we'd think of inspiration, we'd conjure up images of muses and other divinities whispering fantastic imaginings in our ears. Today, we still tend to think of inspiration as emanating from outside us. Moments of high creativity are often described as a feeling of being directed by an unknown power that takes you over and controls your mind and body. Space, time, other people, the real world all seem to disappear. However, it's essential to understand that what takes over is *you*, albeit a different part of you than is generally in control.

During a moment of inspiration a delicate balance is struck between your ego, your sense of self, and your unconscious. Most of your ego must be submerged in order for you to discover your intuitive gifts, but just enough ego remains to keep you functional. At these moments it is your unconscious, with its messages and ideas, that has the upper hand. This sort of balance is not often achieved, but at its height, lucid dreams and visionary states are its closest relatives. That's why the experience often feels foreign and otherworldly. You can better use this process to your advantage if you demystify inspiration and take responsibility and credit for your creativity.

Some people believe that the products of inspiration are born fully formed and that their ideas, especially their great ones, are lying somewhere waiting for them. To them, creativity entails searching for the perfect idea and then expressing it in their own way. They become discouraged and self-doubting when a beautiful creation doesn't instantly pop out of them like a soufflé out of an oven. Although creativity may occasionally work that way, most of the time it doesn't. Ideas form and germinate in our unconscious mind, which has a structure and language unlike that of the conscious mind. Most of the ideas that survive the many barriers protecting the conscious mind are still in an embryonic form. The unconscious has done its work, and now the conscious mind must use its skills.

We all probably receive many more inspirational gifts than we realize because of this false myth about how those gifts should be packaged. When you are doing the exercises in this book, don't automatically discard ideas that seem "wrong" or "unworkable." In Chapter Four, "It's as Easy as Child's Play," you will learn how to let your conscious mind *play* with them for awhile. You may then fashion something usable or, in the course of your play, your unconscious might come up with an even better structure or format for them.

Another myth about inspiration is that it entails pain. Creative people both great and failed have been victims of the romantic and melodramatic myth that inspiration is inextricably linked to pain. While it is true that emotional pain can be released during the act of creativity, there is also the pain, inertia, and failure that results from not understanding how inspiration actually works. Many people feel blocked, depressed, or irritated right before an idea comes to them. One reason is that while the idea is growing in the unconscious, it can stir deep feelings that we don't understand. This is called the "void before creation" and will be discussed in Chapter Two, "What Stands in Your Way." The void before creation appears to be a creative block, but it is really just the conscious mind emptying itself so that it can receive the gifts of the unconscious. Try thinking of inspiration as a gestation process, similar to a pregnancy. Then imagine having all the symptoms of pregnancy without knowing the reason why. You can be sure that the normal discomfort associated with pregnancy would be magnified at least a hundredfold if you didn't understand that you were pregnant. Unfortunately, this is the way many of us experience our creative process. By understanding the way ideas develop, we can accept the discomforting symptoms as evidence that our unconscious is actually working for us.

Inspiration occurs in the flow of creative energy connecting the unconscious with the conscious. Associations (memories, imaginings, and images) from your conscious mind mix with the storehouse of memories and feelings in your unconscious. Immediately or over time, elements of the two worlds connect and spontaneously combust to form a new unexpected synergistic whole. This new embryonic idea then grows in the unconscious mind until it is sufficiently developed to be used by the conscious mind.

When the idea is ready to surface, it often faces the censorship mechanisms of our conscious mind which protects us and generally fears the unknown. If the idea survives this inspection, it then surfaces, and we experience that wonderful "Ah-ha!" that comes from a new thought popping miraculously into our heads. However, this new idea doesn't always—or even often—emerge in perfect form. It is then up to the conscious mind, working in a fluid two-way connection with the unconscious, to re-shape the idea until the ideal configuration is reached. Remember, you will benefit from your unconscious's contributions if you're open to working with *imperfect* ideas rather than just tossing them aside.

Nothing can replace time in the development of an idea, but nonetheless we don't need to passively wait until the idea emerges of its own accord. We can nurture our unconscious and remove the barriers that block the free and easy passage of ideas from the unconscious to the conscious. The exercises in this book are designed to both stimulate the unconscious and circumvent the conscious mind's judgments.

These exercises have developed out of proven methods of business people, artists, inventors, and scholars, as well as from my own work with patients and students. They are also based on my personal exploration in painting and writing. *Creative Breakthroughs* is a natural outgrowth of my previous book, *The Dream Workbook*, which was dedicated to discovering the knowledge and power hidden in dreams. *Creative Breakthroughs* takes you on a further journey, assisting you in summoning forth your innate creativity from the depths of your being. The book is based on the belief that you can heighten your creativity during your waking life as well as your dreaming life—and that each can intensify and enrich the other.

The exercises bypass your defenses by taking you off-guard. They go beyond the barriers of the conscious mind. In that way you can open up to the murky, beautiful richness inside. You will learn how to unearth the seeds of creativity during your waking hours and then utilize your dreams for further discovery at night. The book is sprinkled with numerous examples and anecdotes of both the famous and the "ordinary-but-not-so-ordinary" folk you will meet in these pages. I believe that each of you reading this book can also learn to tap your unconscious.

In a systematic step-by-step program, *Creative Breakthroughs* invites you to participate in the twenty-eight exercises that put you in touch with the innate creativity that lies within. Each exercise is accompanied by examples of people who did the exercises and how they benefited from them. Sometimes the results are sudden and dramatic; more often they are cumulative. After completing one of the creativity workshops, a college administrator reported:

> What has changed for me essentially is that I have a source of self—a bank of senses and expressions and feelings and instincts and a willingness to express them and to risk doing that.

It's just absolutely and entirely new. There's a
storehouse of material there, which wasn't there
before. . . . I dare to do stuff instead of procras-
tinating, weighing it out, haggling about it and
fretting. I just do it. . . . I got in touch with oceans
of things which I didn't know were there—unconscious images. I'm less paranoid, more trusting. I like looking at people straight in the eye,
I'm less frightened. And I have more fun.

A middle-aged computer consultant whose children are
now grown confessed:

I got in touch with the importance of waking
up to myself . . . and things that I always buried
and buried and buried. With the kids, the house,
I didn't have time. Now that I made the time,
it's been an adventure waking up to myself. Since
I started this workshop, I've tried a lot of different
things. It's really helped me to look within
myself—I see why I procrastinated all the time
when I wanted to start something. Now I just
plunge in with both feet, and I don't care if it
doesn't come out well.

Some students report getting to areas never touched before
through years of therapy; almost all acknowledge increased self-knowledge and awareness. This new self-
awareness empowers them to make decisions and take
risks that can enrich their daily lives. This is what creativity
is about: living fully aware, intensely in contact with the
richness of self, and open to the world of experience.

In Part One of this book, you will begin to activate your
unconscious mind by doing Exercise 1, "Where would
you like to be six months from now?" This exercise, which

appears at the end of this chapter, triggers Stage Two of the creative process: *incubation*. The exercises that follow will intensify the process by making you aware of your creative blocks and conflicts. You will examine your fears of failure and success, thus bringing these barriers to the fore. Other exercises will stimulate your creativity through play, fantasy, humor, and dialogues with the child that lives, usually hidden, within you. All the exercises are easy, practical, and fun to do.

In Part Two of the book, you will learn much more about the *incubation* process. You will discover what it is, how it works, and the effects of asking your dreams for the answers to problems or resolutions to conflicts. One man who felt his life was at a standstill asked his dream what to do about it. That night he dreamt he was running as hard and as fast as he could, but (just as in life) he didn't get anywhere. In the dream he changed the angle of his body while he was running, so that now he was at a forward inclination rather than upright as before. Suddenly the houses became a blur as he found himself racing through the streets, covering large expanses quickly and without effort. He mused over the dream upon awakening and began to understand its meaning. The dream was telling him he was dwelling on the present with all its disappointments rather than focusing on his future goals where he could make great strides. Within minutes he began to glimpse different solutions to his life.

Part Three of the book will introduce three newly created exercises for instant insights and will also show you how to change a negative reality from a minus to a plus. While the exercises sometimes provide an immediate insight that you can incorporate into your life without difficulty, at other times you may be required to take an active risk.

Part Four of the book discusses the benefits of taking risks and the powerful effects of creativity and dreaming on your life. Finally, after working through these exercises, you will discover just how much closer you are to your original objectives—and you will be able to set new ones. You will also learn how to maintain yourself in the creative mode so that life continues to unfold its riches and wonders.

Keeping a journal is a very important part of the process. Let your journal be your workbook—your chronicle of discovery. Include in it all your exercises, as well as all the bits of inspiration and new ideas that you experience during this process. You may also want to enter any imagery that inspires you: photographs, drawings, poetry, and dreams, your own or others'. This is your special book, your work in progress. Now let me give you a few words of caution. One of the first *don'ts* of creativity is don't strive for perfection, because your preconception about what is perfect is a formidable barrier that stops your creativity. More *don'ts*: don't be afraid of the ugly or the trivial. Don't censor your thoughts or impulses. What's important is the process. Include in your journal everything that has meaning to you at that instant, regardless of how it looks.

Select a journal that pleases you: consider the color, size, weight, texture of the pages. You can paste words, pictures, or a collage on the cover. Make it as personal as possible. Once you begin your creative journey, you can refer to your journal at any time you need motivation or new ideas, or wish to feel inspired. Later you can flip back through the pages and have the pleasure of observing your creativity unfold.

Exercise 1:
WHERE WOULD YOU LIKE TO BE
SIX MONTHS FROM NOW?

Begin the process now by writing your response to this question in your journal. Try covering all the essential areas of your life in full detail: your creativity, your work, your relationships, the way you live your life, your accomplishments, etc. Don't dilute the effects by considering whether your wishes are possible or not. Once you begin releasing your imagination and taking risks, you'll be surprised how much is possible. So write down your description of *you*—six months from today, living the life you want to live.

2

WHAT STANDS IN YOUR WAY

What stands in the way of your creativity? If you plead laziness, that's simply another way of saying you're blocked. Blocks are obstructions to the free flow of energy. They can be temporary, inconvenient frustrations; or they can drag on for years, impediments to a lifetime of creative expression. Many of us experience blocks in different aspects of our lives: in our jobs, careers, studies, and relationships as well as in creative pursuits. These blocks often do not leave of their own volition, but approaching them head-on is not the way to overcome them either. We have to sneak up behind our blocks and *use* them as an energy source for whatever it is we hope to accomplish. The exercises in this chapter provide a means to transform obstacles into opportunities for creative expression and problem solving.

A wide array of feelings and experiences may be inhibiting your creative expression and success. For the sake of convenience, I have separated these conditions into three broad categories: resistance, immobilization, and the void before creation.

RESISTANCE

Resistance is a case of "We know what we would like to do, but we don't know how to do it." Or we have the idea but can't get ourselves to the typewriter, computer, easel, library, etc., to work on it. At the thought of heading off to create, a hundred chores pop up. "Practical" tasks are a popular choice of the unconscious since most of us have been conditioned to believe it's more important to take care of them than to tend to our creativity. Cleaning house, doing the laundry, shopping for food, even rearranging the furniture can suddenly become imperative "must-do's." Once-repugnant tasks can take on a new light; sometimes it seems we'll do almost anything to avoid throwing ourselves into the creative unknown. The unconscious can be highly creative in the ways it fashions our modes of resistance and makes up rationales for them. One painter wryly notes that if it weren't for her work, she'd probably never clean the toilet.

Of course, once all the chores are done, there simply isn't enough time or energy left for our creativity. We may feel somewhat guilty but no one can say we've been unproductive; our photos had to be pasted into the album some time! The way we use our time, and our tendency to feel that we don't have enough of it, are great allies of resistance.

Not all resistances take the form of onerous tasks; other desires and urges can seduce us away from our creativity as well. For many people there's nothing like the notion of doing something creative to bring out the yawns and send them trotting off for a nap. Others develop voracious appetites that can only be satiated by hours of rummaging through the refrigerator. An engineer who wanted desperately to change careers stopped working on his résumé for a while because it was making him gain too much weight. Sex, television, crossword puzzles, and exercise are other popular diversions. We make bargains with ourselves: "I'll start working on my project as soon as I finish reading this chapter," or "once this television show is over," or "I'll work all day tomorrow if I can see this movie today."

Before we can combat these resistances, we have to understand their roots as well as their manifestations. Almost everyone faced with a task feels the task is too difficult or that there isn't enough time to complete it. Ironically the most productive people often have the least time. The use and management of time are much more flexible than most of us imagine, once we make up our minds to regard our creative pursuits as *the* priority. Understanding why you resist, coupled with an acknowledgement that your creative goals are more important than many "practical" concerns, can enable you to make the compromises in your lifestyle and use of time that will dramatically improve your life. You may, for example, be able to totally absorb yourself in your creative activity even though your car needs to be washed or your favorite television show is on.

In most instances time is more an excuse than a reason; once the real cause of the resistance is uncovered and resolved, time often ceases to be a big problem. One major cause of resistance is lacking the conviction that what you are doing or are about to do is worthwhile and meaningful. This triggers a "So what?" response to your ideas. "So what?" is a very effective barrier to creativity; it relieves you of the responsibility of pursuing a particular direction. This attitude is fueled by the sense that everything has already been done or said, and nothing that we do is new and thus worthwhile. We compare ourselves to others who have explored the same territory, judge our own contribution as inferior or lacking, and dismiss the entire project with a "Why bother?" To some extent it is true that there are very few totally new ideas, but that isn't the point. Opening ourselves up to new experiences, discovering new truths about ourselves and life, moving other people and touching their emotions, enjoying the exhilaration of the creative process—these are the objectives of most creative expression. If you can develop your own fresh perspective on an idea and implement it or communicate it in a novel way that has some impact, it doesn't matter if it's been done before.

Fear of failure and of disappointing yourself and others can also interfere with your sticking with a project or idea. Do you have an audience in mind when you are creating? Is it your family, a special person, a special group of people, many people, yourself? You may find you have too many people psychologically looking over your shoulder, or you may be trying to satisfy someone who is impossible to please or apathetic about your creativity. What is it you're trying to get from your creativity? One woman who was about to start a new business realized that it was just another attempt to win the love she had never received from her parents. She blamed herself for this, and the blame contributed to her feeling of resistance. If you're trying to use your creativity to get something that isn't a natural by-product of it, you most likely will end up disappointed. Many people build up grandiose fantasies around themselves and their creativity, and the fear of not fulfilling these fantasies by being perfect stops them from trying. Here again it's important to explore your need for perfection and what you believe it will bring you. Your feelings about your creative process can be the root of the resistance. It's important to enjoy the process; the approval and praise you're seeking won't fill you by themselves, no matter how much you get.

Exercises 2–8 at the end of the chapter will guide you in discovering and resolving the conflicts that bring on your resistances in your creativity, so that you will be able to derive more enjoyment and productivity.

IMMOBILIZATION

When you feel immobilized, everything is gone: your ideas, your talent, your motivation. Immobilization, which can last anywhere from a few days to many years, provokes great anguish for the person who wishes to be creative; and the pain and loss of self-esteem can cause the immobilization to be self-perpetuating. After writing twenty-four operas and enjoying great acclaim, Giuseppe Verdi declared there were no more operatic melodies in his head. He reverted to being a gentleman farmer and was dry for fourteen years. Then, near the end of his life, he wrote the opera *Otello*, and six years later, the opera *Falstaff*. He died shortly thereafter.

Many of us feel immobilized just at the point when we have a great idea. And for those who have had productive periods in the past, it is a major source of frustration. Immobilization occurs for many reasons. The death of a loved one often brings on a dearth of productivity that may last a very long time. One woman stopped painting for seven years after her father died and only picked up the brush again after joining a creativity workshop and working through some of her conflicts. Immobilization can be a way of misbehaving and being "bad," and a method of punishing ourselves by saying we don't deserve to be creative. Very often the causes of immobilization are not immediately apparent; they involve our deepest feelings and frequently relate to childhood experiences.

While some people suffer a single block that goes on for an extended period of time, others find that blocks crop up and disappear in their lives with varying frequency. Sometimes we go through dry periods where nothing seems to interest us; we may be in a mild depression without realizing it. However, creativity ironically is also a way out of the depression. One school of psychoanalytic thought believes that creativity is a way back to the self: this is based upon the premise that as infants we disown parts of ourselves in order to survive, and creative expression restores these lost parts and makes us whole once more.

Understanding the underlying causes of your block is helpful. Another approach is to look at your block from a *practical point of view*: recall your past blocks and the events both leading up to them and preceding their disappearance. Are there patterns? Getting this kind of overview of your blocks can indicate how they were resolved, and this, in turn, can facilitate your dealing with current and future blocks.

The exercises provided in this chapter are meant to elude your inner barriers and provide a forum for your block to reveal itself. They arouse the conflicting tensions within you, which is an essential step in overcoming blocks. In an apparent paradox, you use the block that stops you from creating as the inspirational energy with which to create. In addition, the exercises automatically put you in the realm of doing, which is the opposite of being blocked. This can be a first step toward overcoming the block, even if the block is a deep one that's persisted for years.

THE VOID BEFORE CREATION

The void before creation is a common yet little-understood phenomenon. Almost every creative person knows that frustrating emptiness. The will is there; the paint, paper, typewriter, word processor, video camera, telephone lie there waiting to be used; everything is present except our ability to do something with those materials. The elusive creative power seems to have deserted us, and try as we may, nothing comes out: no words, images, thoughts, sounds. Our storehouse of ideas seems empty. Or else we struggle with confusion or fragments, often contradictory, that don't fit together into a whole and seem to lead nowhere. This is one way in which an adult's creativity differs from that of a child, for creativity comes naturally to children, without effort or intentional thought.

However, this feeling of emptiness, this void, often precedes great creativity. It can be a period of gestation, when ideas take form in our unconscious until they're sufficiently developed to be usable by the conscious mind. Like a pregnant woman about to give birth, we're often uncomfortable and restless, but unfortunately we don't always know what's causing that feeling. It then becomes very easy for the concern over *when* we'll be creative to swell to an anxiety over *if* we'll ever be creative again.

The concept of the void before creation is prevalent in

many forms. Eastern religion describes the void before reaching "satori" (total enlightenment). According to the Bible, there was *nothing* before God created the universe. A basic law of physics states that two things cannot occupy the same place at the same time. If a glass is filled with water, you must empty it before it can be filled with wine. And, in doing so, there will be a period of time, seconds or hours, when the glass will be empty. It's the same with creativity. It's as if that which feels like a void is really our conscious mind emptying itself so that it can be filled by the ideas germinating in our unconscious.

Thus, the void before creation is not really a block or resistance even though it often feels like one; in itself it is a viable initial stage of the creative process. How can you determine if this is what's happening to you? First, examine your previous patterns. Do you often have periods of emptiness followed by great creative activity? Are you at the beginning of a new project or idea? Look at the different phases of your creative process.

You can enhance this period of creative gestation, thereby giving your unborn idea nourishment and making the process less difficult. The first step is to acknowledge that you're *not* blocked and are, in fact, engaged in the creative process. This goes a long way toward alleviating much of the anxiety and discomfort triggered by the sense of the void. This is the time to nurture yourself by exposing yourself to creative stimulation. Since your ideas are forming in the unconscious, that is a good place to focus your energy and attention. Your dreams are direct paths to the unconscious. The process of incubation, whereby the unconscious mind continues to work on a problem even after the conscious mind has stopped, often reveals its contributions in jokes, slips of the tongue, and unprovoked images. Psychoanalyst Rollo May explained in his book *The Courage To Create* that answers to problems come when the mind is at rest, especially in areas in which the person has worked "laboriously and with dedication." Our neurological thought processes continue even when we're asleep.[1]

If you feel the birth of your idea is long overdue, it may be that you're overly critical of your idea in its raw form and expect it to come out perfectly the first time. This kind of self-criticism kills creative spontaneity. Let's now move on to unblocking our blocks.

Exercise 2:
DIALOGUE BETWEEN CONFLICTING ELEMENTS

Nobody is completely free from conflict. The conflicts which cause the most trouble in our creativity may center around self-esteem. You may have a conflict about your desire to fully express yourself and the fear of rejection and ridicule; or a conflict between what you consider to be your true value versus the reactions of others. A good way to explore and resolve these feelings is to write a conversation between the two conflicting elements—for example, your creative side and your logical side—or between your desires and your fears; between what you "can" do and what you "can't" do; between the part of you that feels like a success and the part that feels like a failure; between perfection and imperfection.

Write the dialogue spontaneously, without censoring yourself. Let each side fully express its opinions and feelings until you come to some kind of resolution. What does each side see as the problems? As the priorities? Determining the root of the conflict and exploring all the feelings fighting for attention are the first steps toward resolving it.

A painter wrote this conversation between her desires and her fears regarding her work:

DESIRES: I'm surprised that I'm as proud as I used to be ten years ago, and more so. I don't have any doubts about how good my work is and how good I am.

FEARS: That's a laugh. You always had doubts. When others told you you were good, you never believed them. They had to tell you fifty times. Aren't you afraid that you're a fraud? That you don't know what you're doing? That you made some devil's pact so you could fool people? Aren't you afraid that you're bad or evil? Or at least that you'll be forced to be bad and be punished, to pay the devil for the good work and the recognition? You want that praise too much.

DESIRES: Yes, and I want to create work that surprises. Shockingly beautiful. Magical! What color! What statements! I do want them.

FEARS: Stay away from magic, it can destroy you. It's bad to try for the things you want to realize. You'll have to pay. You'll be caught and be humiliated. Caught red-handed, stealing.

DESIRES: It isn't stealing. It's mine. Why should I have to pay for what I make? Who's helping me? Nobody. It's mine. I do it all myself. I have a right to be me.

Afterward, she said, "I suddenly realized that I must have been punished for showing off. I never thought about it before, but showing my paintings to others is showing off. So I got to thinking about showing off as a kid . . . boasting and that sort of thing. I probably was an exhibitionist."

She learned that this negative perception of herself was fueling her block.

A high school teacher who couldn't motivate himself to do the thing he really loved—photography—was having a hard time channeling his abundant energy. He wrote this conversation between his logical side and his creative side.

CREATIVE SIDE: I think you're holding me back. I want to explore new areas, try new things. And you're always there with your judgments: "It's not commercial." "Someone already did that." "You'll never sell that." "You're wasting your time." You sound like my mother, telling me to go to computer programmer school. You drain my energy and excitement.

LOGICAL SIDE: Give me a break. If it wasn't for me you'd never get anything done. You're a genius in the bathtub, but I'm the one who gets you to the camera. Judging from your output . . .

CREATIVE SIDE: See, there you go again. "Judging."

LOGICAL SIDE: Well, someone's got to look at what's going on and evaluate it. You say you want to do certain things, but I'm not the one holding you back; you are, with your laziness. I say fine, go ahead and do whatever creative thing you want, but do it, don't just think about how wonderful it will be getting recognition for it. I'm the lost child here, and I feel like I'm trying to control a two-ton elephant, or better yet, a two-ton diva. You ain't going nowhere without me, look at where you are now! Are you happy, fulfilled, where you think you should be?

CREATIVE SIDE: No.

LOGICAL SIDE: Well, why do you think that is? Don't blame me, I have almost no control over you.

CREATIVE SIDE: I feel if you take control, or even have equal power, I'll disappear. The magic will be gone.

LOGICAL SIDE: You would think that. Magic has nothing to do with it. I'm telling you, you're not weak and fragile, needing constant nurturing. That may be a nice romantic image, but with you, it ain't true. You're running the show and you're a lousy administrator, self-indulgent and everything. You're trying to do too much, to do what I'm supposed to do as well as your own job. And never, never listening to me. Why don't you just let me do my job, huh? Believe it or not, I can help you. Not by giving you ideas or judging your work, God forbid, but helping to motivate you, getting you to actually do it, accomplish it. You waste so much time, you manage time terribly—reading all those magazines and having to watch two and a half hours of news every night. You, who comes back from your teaching and doesn't even leave the house, are so consumed by what's happening millions of miles away. I could help you get your work done, so you could do even more things. We don't have a partnership, and I'll tell you, it's hurting you more than it's hurting me.

CREATIVE SIDE: This makes me nervous. I don't know how to let you out, when to let you out.

LOGICAL SIDE: Why don't you let me decide that?

CREATIVE SIDE: Oh no!

LOGICAL SIDE: Why not? I'm sure I'd be a better boss than you are. And you'll always be stronger than me, so you can always take over again.

CREATIVE SIDE: I feel that if I let you take over, and rule me, I'll lose what's special about me, and I'll be weak.

LOGICAL SIDE: You'll never be weak, and I'm no threat. I'm practically atrophied from disuse. And you won't be any less special. No one has to know I'm running things. As long as you do what I say, you can still pretend to be the same lunatic. You'll just have more to show for it. I can serve you. Don't think of me as a boss, think of me as a highly efficient executive secretary, or assistant. Everyone has those people, nudging them, getting them from one place to the next. They never get any credit, but without them the big wheels would never get anything done.

CREATIVE SIDE: You know why this idea scares me? It's funny, I never thought I felt this way; but listening to you, and knowing that what you say makes sense and would work for me, and yet at the same time feeling terribly resistant, makes me think that I'm afraid of success, or maybe afraid of failure. Operating on my own at least allows me the delusion that I'm not working at full capacity, and that's why I'm not getting where I want. But if you became part of this too, and I'm really committing everything and still not going anywhere . . . I don't know if I could take that.

LOGICAL SIDE: I'm not going to lie to you: that's true. I don't think that will happen, but if it does, you will be sad. But, on the other hand, if you don't try you're going to end up bitter because you didn't really give yourself a full chance.

CREATIVE SIDE: You got it.

He indeed found that allowing his logical side to have an active administrative role in his creative process got him to do his photography, rather than just dream about it.

Exercise 3:
VISUALIZE YOUR BLOCK

The unconscious often speaks most eloquently through pictures; dreams are a dramatic example of this. Visualizing your block will enable hidden aspects of it to emerge from the unconscious.

As you picture your block, describe it in as much detail as possible. Expand upon it, let it speak for itself about its experiences and its past, examine its texture. Creatively expressing this visualization is another way to transform your block from a handicap into a tool. If you have difficulty forming a mental picture of your block, try free associating to it first and let the image form from that.

A public relations executive envisioned her block as a mirrored maze and wrote this description of it:

> I walk into the maze, the maze of past possibilities, past realities, past creations. Not the meadow of spontaneity where ideas can run free and grow as they will. The maze is concerned with restriction and boundaries, holding ideas up to banal comparisons that trip the ever-vulnerable impulse. In the maze I can constantly turn in any direction and see my flaws and faults, and it seems to amplify them as well. Every angle, every turn, seems to hold up to my creative urge a squareness of ideas, a predictability of product.

In the maze there is no air; staleness aborts my attempts at vain greatness.

But free from the maze, in the freshness and expansiveness of the grassy hilltop, I am not face to face with vanity or even limits. Looking away frees the mind, liberates the spirit, and that which I know *is* may take its own flight.

In consciously making a point to get herself out of the maze and experiencing those sensations, she realized that the way out of her block was to momentarily step away from the problem and free herself from the staleness she had created. In this way the ideas within her would have a chance to grow and surface.

Drawing your block also provides new insights. Although an artist drew the following example, "Gridlock at the Champs-Elysées" (Figure 1), you don't have to be an artist to do this exercise. It can work for anyone. Back to the artist, however. Underneath the picture he wrote: "Ideas charging in from all sides until it's so busy and cluttered that the center becomes blank and empty and confused." He described the jumbled mess as "madness, a cacophony of horns blaring, but no one moving." He felt that a policeman was needed to direct traffic, to say which cars should go where and when. He then realized that he could never handle the traffic jam of his ideas that way; he'd take too long to make decisions and constantly change his mind anyway. The best way to direct the traffic jam, he said, was to go up in a helicopter and view it from above, the way he had drawn it in his picture. He saw that the best way for him to deal with the ideas blocked in his mind was to get an overview, a broad picture of them and their general direction, rather than trying to decide the merit of each idea.

A social worker whose secret desire was to be a painter

#3
A picture of my creative block.

Gridlock at The
Champs d'Elysee's.

Ideas charging in from all sides
until it's so busy and cluttered that in the
center it all becomes blank and empty and confused

Figure 1

drew this picture of her many-tentacled block, "The World" (Figure 2), and drew a minuscule stick figure of herself at the bottom saying, "Give me a break." Each of the tentacles is one manifestation of the block. Starting at the top and moving clockwise are: A broken screwdriver—broken equipment; the cost of art supplies; the art gallery saying, "No, we can't use your work;" cleaning my apartment; doing the dishes; people who say mean things; people who say, "We don't like your artwork;" people who say, "Worse, we have nothing to say about your artwork;" myself; work that I do for money that gets in the way; being given a bad space to put my work once I do get a gallery; getting other people to do their jobs right; getting phone numbers from Information and always having to make toll calls; and when it's all put together, the feeling that I can't make it.

She saw that all these individual blocks were small, and that there was plenty of room in her drawing for her to slip by them. After doing the exercise she remarked, "What I understand about this block is that it's really an opportunity for me to push past it and be that much better. This block is impressive but it's also vulnerable."

A young sales manager who hated writing reports, an important part of his job, envisioned his block as an ugly, green, reptilian man covered with warts who blocks the way to his success. After drawing a picture of it (Figure 3), he wrote this regarding the block: "Work = heavy, thick, earth/water, ugly, demanding effort, heavy-handed, fun-quashing, old/straight." About himself he wrote: "Me = light, free, air/fire, floaty, wanting to sail without effort, footloose, fiercely independent, young, rebellious."

As he reviewed the characteristics of his block, he initially concluded that he didn't like its qualities and thus felt no great urge to get past it. If being a success represented those traits, he wanted no part of it. He would be

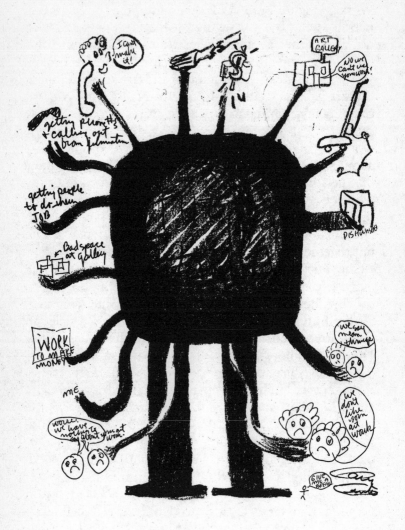

Figure 2

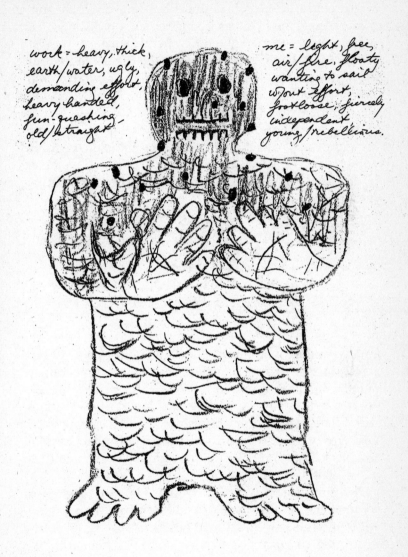

Figure 3

better off in a different field. But as he examined his picture more closely his feelings changed. His block appeared more comical than frightening. To his surprise, he discovered that he liked it and sensed that he could use this block. He realized that it was much more aggressive than he was, and thus could be the vehicle for him to make it. He commented, "The whole idea of a block is a lighter thing for me now. It's not that much bigger than me anymore, and I can choose whether or not to do anything about it. I can play with it now instead of being frustrated by it and feeling like a victim of it. Maybe work can be fun."

Exercise 4:
WRITE THE SITUATION FROM THE BLOCK'S POINT OF VIEW

In any conflict, you must understand your opponent before you can disarm or defeat him or her; and this is equally applicable to our battles with creative blocks. Blocks and resistances are messages; we must understand these messages in order to resolve the blocks. Once the concerns of the unconscious are uncovered and addressed, the block loses its purpose, its reason for being, and thus can be laid to rest.

A simple, direct way to decipher a block's message is to, in effect, become the block and write out the situation from its perspective. Making your block a separate entity with its own voice gives you enough psychological distance from it that those thoughts and feelings that usually are submerged can come forth. At the same time, it enables you to directly experience and release the feelings surrounding your block. As with all of the exercises, it's imperative to write spontaneously, without censoring yourself. If you have trouble getting started, ask your block, "Why are you here?" or "How do you perceive this situation?" and go from there. Often through this you can learn how your block operates and what it's trying to do.

A woman who longed to be noticed and to be sought after always kept herself very safe in social situations and personal relationships. She gave voice to her block:

> I am Elaine's block. I'm here to say that it's not an easy job. She is continually trying to make an impression on people. I am about staying safe, small, unnoticed, sheltered. I want the status quo. I like every day being the same as the next. I know what to look forward to; I can even plan what scares me. It's like being a candle that goes lower and lower until it burns out.
>
> If I had my way, the context of Elaine's life would be no light, and grimness would prevail. Storms would be brewing perpetually.
>
> The pay-off is complete and perfect control. I made it, I have it, and I will never change. I will stay in my shell. No one can get in. Complete stasis, impossible in nature but I can create it. She will never escape me. I don't need joy. *She* does. Those items of comfort and pleasure are her toys, trying to distract me from my purpose. She is weak. Therefore I am the one who will win.

Afterward, the woman commented that it was a little frightening that the block had such a formulated and persevering point of view. She saw how her need for safety and control not only fueled her block in personal relationships but stood in the way of a successful career as well. She wanted to search for ways to satisfy these needs without compromising herself.

Another woman who had many creative interests but never pursued any of them gave voice to her block with this result:

> I keep Janet on a treadmill. I hardly ever give her a chance to do what she wants. I keep her busy every night of the week and on weekends. I keep her tired and throw obligations at her so fast that I don't know how she gets anything done. I keep her away from other creative people because of her job, and when she does see them I make sure she feels like an imposter or that they are hostile to her. Lately she's been friendly with a few; that makes her too comfortable, she feels like she belongs. I'd better give her a few scares so that she'll retreat again from being herself and so feel alienated again. I'm trying to make her fail by tiring her, discouraging her, keeping her away from or afraid of other creative people, and what she thinks they think of her. When she was younger I used her father's fear that she would starve to death, or worse, make a fool of herself.

The experience of having her block present its terrorizing tactics so clearly and directly greatly lessened their impact on her.

A woman who studied singing all her life but never performed wrote:

> I am Bonnie's fear. I have put a cage around her. I prevent her from moving freely. I love to hurt her. She's incapable of doing things well so

I stand in her way. I rip her apart if she so much as sticks her hand out of the cage. I'll teach her. She's going to suffer if she dares. Supposing I let her out. Then I wouldn't have a hold on her. She would be free of me; she would have the upper hand. I will always be in control and make the decisions. I know what is right and how things should be. People shouldn't try to be more than they were meant to be. And in this case I know what's best. If I let her go her own way, she's only going to get herself in a worse state. I'm here to keep tabs on her, to make sure she doesn't get too outrageous or cocky or self-centered. And heaven forbid, what if she embarrassed me? She doesn't know her own mind.

After writing this she remarked, "As I was doing this I suddenly realized that I was writing from my father's voice. And yet there was another side of him, encouraging me and buying me everything. There's a conflict between these two things, two impressions he gave me." Through this exercise she saw how much she had internalized her father's unspoken but powerful feelings regarding her self-expression.

Many people are unconsciously dealing with parental attitudes that block their creativity. In Exercise 6 you will conjure up the voice of that inner critical parent.

Exercise 5:
PICTURE YOURSELF IN A SITUATION YOU'RE APPREHENSIVE ABOUT; THEN REPLACE YOUR NEGATIVE THOUGHTS WITH POSITIVE ONES

This young woman was putting herself through college and was looking for a part-time job. The perfect one appeared in a newspaper advertisement. It was an assistant's job in the admissions office of a university and would be an ideal way to subsidize her college education, since courses for employees were free. She made an appointment for an interview and was exceedingly nervous about the impression she would make:

> When I meet Mrs. White, I'll extend my hand and say, "How nice to meet you, Mrs. White." The first thing she'll notice is that my clothing looks shabby, and that I don't dress well. She'll probably think I'm poor. (She's right!) She'll think I have no sense of style. She'll also notice my awkwardness. Suppose she asks me for previous experience. I'll have to lie and say I've worked for companies longer than I really have. I can't tell her that I was fired from my last job. And I don't even know why. I was polite. I was never late. For some reason they didn't like me, and I never was able to find out why, since they just let me go without an explanation. Maybe they thought I seemed unfriendly. I didn't talk to people much, because I was afraid to. Mrs.

White may have the same opinion about me they
did.

This young woman realized she was always forming negative pictures in her mind whenever she had to meet a
new challenge or situation. She decided to try something
different, to substitute positive pictures for the negative
ones. She was able to form a picture that totally replaced
the previous ones, and this enabled her to make an excellent impression at her interview. The picture was a
composite of all the positive impressions she had had of
herself at different times of her life, fleeting though they
were: as a pretty, gracious person, eager to do a good job,
honest in her enthusiasm, and intelligent. It was through
the image, the picture—not the words—that she was able
to change her attitude. Forming a vivid picture in your
mind of positive past self-impressions can have a powerful
influence on your performance.

Exercise 6:
CONJURE UP YOUR INNER
CRITICAL PARENT

So much of our self-esteem is based on the attitudes our
parents had toward us when we were children. This is
crucial because our self-esteem, or lack thereof, can affect
whether or not we persist in a creative goal. Many people
discover, when doing this exercise, that it is the negative
voice of a parent or both parents that blocks them from
success. This is the story of an office manager who desperately wanted to do artwork. In this exercise, she con-

jured up her family's voice by allowing herself to reflect back on all the times she had done something creative. This exercise, she reported, gave her insight into her block and encouraged her to do her art anyway. In her words:

> I discovered that for me my art work is to get all the approval and love that I never got. And it's too threatening for me to put this out and be rejected. It was just too painful. And when I created, at some level (although I never realized it at the time and thought I was doing it for myself), deep down I know now it was to get everything that I never got . . . I used to get a lot of negative comments at home. One time I did a woodblock for a Christmas card, and I worked all night doing it. I ran up to show it to my mother and she said, "What are you making such a fuss for? Five dollars and you can go out and buy Christmas cards!"
>
> Last summer I had a chance to be in a show, but I didn't have any work. I really had to struggle to do all this work within two weekends. I went to the country, upstate where my mother and brother lived. And I worked like crazy in the basement. My mother passed by, and then my brother. And they never once looked at what I was doing or asked to see what I was doing. It was really like the ultimate rejection . . . Now just realizing that I have all this anger and all this negativity is a breakthrough for me. What else could I expect when my background and my history were so bad! Just recognizing that I have these feelings and they're not my fault gives me the courage to go through them. I always have a tendency to blame everything on me—"Oh, if only I had done this better." I know now I don't

have to keep dwelling on it and continue to be negative. The fact that I can say, "Hey, listen, it really was bad." And the fact that I have even survived this far is a tribute to myself. It's a real step for me.

Sometimes the inner voices are not critical, but nevertheless are stifling. A market researcher commented: "My family thought everything I did was wonderful, even things I knew I wasn't good at. So therefore I have this inability to trust what I really believe I'm good at. Like they'd say I was a fabulous athlete; I never was. And you know, that could be just as bad."

Not only can we be affected by the way our parents view our creativity, but we can be equally influenced by negative examples our parents set for us. An architect, who could only rely on tools of the trade and could never break loose to create something fresh, spoke about his father as a very technical man. "And my mother," he said, "was sort of failed as an artist. I just realized that may be very much a part of all my problems; she always started creating, she started painting, she does weaving, all those things—but she never gets anywhere."

These insights can set the stage for change.

Exercise 7:
BRAG ABOUT YOURSELF; THEN
HAVE A DIALOGUE WITH THE VOICE
THAT DISPUTES YOU

Most of us have no problem belittling our creativity, and even ourselves on occasion; but complimenting ourselves is an entirely different story. Our self-doubts can make it difficult to trust other people's appreciation of who we are and what we do and can keep us from truly valuing ourselves. This persistent questioning of our abilities subverts our motivation, spontaneity, and ability to take risks and experiment; resistances thrive in this atmosphere. Before we can regain our drained power we must confront these doubts.

Bragging about yourself and your work is a surefire way to get your self-doubts to leap out in full, sharp detail. Write out a thorough, comprehensive explanation of how you are the greatest person, lover, friend, writer, cook, mother, father, executive, etc., in the whole world. Go all the way with this: exaggerate, fantasize, even lie. Push past your inclinations to qualify these compliments or disparage yourself.

By the time you finish writing the first part of this exercise, an inner voice will probably be shrieking "liar" and other insults at you. Now address this voice by writing out a dialogue with *it*; allow it to fully articulate its anger and opinions. This is the voice of your barrier; the more it can express itself directly, the less need it has to act out. Intermixed with the insults can be helpful advice.

A woman, agonizing over having just turned thirty, did the exercise:

> I am wonderful. I'm extremely attractive. I'm striking. And believe it or not, I'm also extremely intelligent. I'm fun to be with. Men are so attracted to me. I'm very sexy. I'm extremely capable. I can be anything I want to be. I'm so talented. No one can stand it, actually.

(The negating voice that then emerged was that of her sister, who had had many problems and had died a few years earlier. The woman had always felt that she had to inhibit herself, not be her real self, because she had to protect her sister from the force of her personality. She then continued bragging.)

> I'm very gregarious. I'm not in the least insecure or shy. I'm brilliant mathematically. I am so, Mom (to a second negating voice). My mind never fouls up. I don't need to rely on anyone. I'm thoroughly capable. I can draw incredibly well, very realistically. I can also play randomly and create stunning things. I could write a novel if I wanted. I sometimes get bored and lose my attention span because it's not interesting or challenging enough. I never put myself down. At least ten men are in love with me. I'm very wealthy. I have just as much power as I decide to have. There's absolutely nothing to criticize about me. Who can criticize perfection?"

(At that point she again thought of her mother and continued her self-affirmation in spite of her.)

> I'm just so talented. My God, I'm amazing, creative, knowledgeable, learned, fascinating. (But a voice in her head said, "You're always exaggerating." She again thought of her mother. She acknowledged that and then went back to bragging.) I'm thoroughly rooted in reality. I am so able to experience the depth of things, the thrill of things. I make other people feel this intensity too. I have a wonderful smile and handshake. I'm very feminine. People are in awe of me.

When she realized how her family dynamics revealed themselves in this exercise, she termed it "amazing."

A sculptor wrote this boast and followed it up with a dialogue:

> No one can take elements and bring them together the way I can. I have an incredible knack for re-creating a day's mood and feelings, and freezing that time forever. I am at my best when I am working with *many* problems that require several solutions. The joy and pride in my creations come from my ability to solve and resolve the technical problems. I always succeed at everything I do; I always have succeeded. I have never failed at anything. I am the best. Creativity and joy flow into me and out of me.

IT: You will never succeed. You are only second-rate talent. Your work at best is mediocre.

ME: That's not true.

IT: You will never be anything better than middle-class.

ME: That's not true. Life and creation flow through me as never before.

IT: Yeah, ha, ha! Go ahead and try. You'll still always be middle-class. There is always going to be something amiss with you.

ME: I'm working and growing. I've learned and I'm developing. I value life, being creative. I think I am special. I have great ability. I will not be stopped from what I need to do. Nothing or no one will get in my way and prevent me from being and doing what I need to do, not even "it," which is me. I will be the best.

This dialogue revealed to him how huge he had made his prejudice against his background. He felt that no great artist had ever come from middle-class society, that artists were products either of enormous wealth, coddled and given every opportunity for growth . . . or of enormous poverty, with their talents honed by their harsh environment.

He described his childhood as "a big bag that I always carry around with me—all those suburban schools I went to and the little house I grew up in." Deliberating on the feelings elicited by this exercise, he remarked, "The funny thing is that my work is now reflecting that background, and I'm beginning to love it. If this is what I have to carry around with me, then I might as well use my background and be it as best I can."

Exercise 8:
DO SOMETHING BADLY

A leading cause of blocks and resistances is excessive self-criticism. Nothing kills a good idea faster than over-analyzing it before it hits paper. It's so important to let go of the quest for perfection in the initial stages of creation. A fresh idea can always be reworked and refined; it's a lot harder to breathe life back into an idea that's been strangled to death before it's found physical expression.

Most people are terribly afraid of doing something badly, something they don't like. We feel we'll carry this one thing around our necks like an albatross for the rest of our lives. The worst thing we can do in a creative endeavor is decide to abandon the idea. But while we intellectually know this to be true, we continue to rob ourselves of the initial experience of an idea and instead kill it by insisting on doing it perfectly the first time. By the time we put it down on paper, we've often lost sight of what the real gist of the idea had been and deprived ourselves of the opportunity to let the idea develop on its own.

The techniques of editing, polishing, applying the finishing touches are essential *in their place and time*, and that place and time is *after* the idea has been explored spontaneously. Jotting down ideas in the form in which they first occur to you and then moving on without revising them enables the entire concept to emerge in its complete form. Your first idea may just be the precursor to the main point, but you might never discover that point if you stop to perfect that initial idea. Newborn ideas evaporate easily, so do these exercises spontaneously, without editing or reworking, so that nothing gets lost.

Since the fear of doing something badly is a leading block to spontaneity, it's important to surmount that barrier. One of the best ways to do that is to consciously do what you're afraid of, what you're trying not to do. Thus, if you pride yourself on being the life of the party, purposely tell a joke badly. If your need is to be extremely fashionable, dress casually instead. If you're afraid of writing bad stories, force yourself to write the worst story you can. If doing a bad drawing keeps your pencil from the paper, see how ugly you can make your picture.

Several interesting things may happen. You may find that it's not as easy to perform as badly as you imagined. Good outcomes and ideas may pop up despite your best (or worst) intentions. You may discover that your innate good taste or your expertise is so ingrained that it doesn't allow you to be too awful. The harder you try to perform badly, the better the task or the work may become. A woman studying flower arranging remarked, "I tried to do bad the best I could and I just sat there for a few minutes; it wouldn't come out bad. And I realized that it was only when I was trying to do well that it came out bad. I saw that it's the mechanism of trying, and self-evaluating and criticizing, that makes something turn out the opposite of what you want."

If you do succeed in doing something truly badly you'll learn that it won't kill you or inalterably ruin you; ideally you'll be able to laugh at it and let it lead you someplace else. While doing this exercise, be aware of the feelings that rise up in you. What does it say about you if you do something badly?

A man who yearned to be a good public speaker always became nervous whenever he faced his audience. One night he was meeting his weekly bowling buddies and he was concerned about the talk he was giving the next day to recruit college students for his corporation. He asked his buddies if he could give them a practice talk, never revealing to them that he was planning to ham it up and make every mistake he was afraid to. And so he did. He stuttered, he exaggerated his stiffness and formality, he made awkward gestures, and he asked the audience composed of his buddies some silly questions. The feedback he got at the end was surprising: his friends found him extremely relaxed and humorous, "not your usual stiff and formal self," they teased him.

A writer set out to write a terrible short story:

A long time ago I was a child alone in a valley. It was a pretty valley, one of orchards and blossoms—and the worst pollen you have ever seen. Sneeze, sneeze, sneeze! from March to June.

At the time I lived with my parents, who resisted being my parents as much as I resisted being their child. They were seldom home and I roamed far and wide. I had a big yellow Labrador with a chewed-up tail and he loved to chase rabbits. We found ourselves frequently in the orchards in the spring, stealing cherries or clipping mustard plants for mysterious teas that the local Indians concocted.

One day, the dog and I discovered an injured muskrat. Muskrats are not indigenous to these parts. The creature put up a pretty good fight with Oscar, my dog, until a girl, somewhat older than I, approached through the yellow mustard blossoms.

"That's my muskrat," she said.

She said it the way a land baron might say he owns acres and acres. I drew back skeptically. You know how the world is. Anybody can come along and say, "Hey, that's my muskrat," just because they want something free and easy.

So I said, "Prove it."

She bent over and murmured to the muskrat, "Harriet, Harriet, what happened? We'll take care of you." Then the girl looked at me poignantly and queried, "Won't we?"

I thought, "Hey wait a minute, I'm not going to be pressured into becoming a foster parent to a muskrat.

"What's your name?" I asked.

"Circa."

I would have asked, "What year?" but being far from knowledgeable then, I asked instead, "Circa what?"

Later we became good friends. Harriet survived and Oscar went on to breed litters of neighborhood pups. Circa ran away the following summer to rescue her father who was in jail in Little Rock, Arkansas.

Afterward she commented, "I had to fight against a very strong urge to edit, but I also felt a great sense of freedom. I felt light and not uptight. I really enjoyed the process of making up the story. I allowed myself to be sentimental, even mediocre, which I don't usually permit, and it wasn't as bad as I thought it would be. I felt a lot more freedom than when I usually write. I didn't have the feeling someone was watching over my shoulder and wonder what their opinion would be. In writing this story I had to go against everything I've been trained in, and it was interesting to see that after years of working there's still a level of professionalism there no matter how bad I try to be or am by accident. Being a critic when you're creating is a real hazard."

This technique is excellent when you're blocked at a certain point in your work or in your life. Deliberately doing a bad rendition of the idea can free you so that the block's grip can loosen and the ideas you want can emerge.

A variation on this idea is to create something in a medium that you're "bad" in. Your censorship mechanisms are generally the fiercest in your area of expertise since this is where your ego has the biggest investment. An excellent way to circumvent them is to express yourself in a different medium. It's easiest to take risks in a medium in which you know, from the outset, that you have little or no ability. Since you're reconciled to never being able to perform in that area, there's no self-esteem at risk and no expectation or pressure to do a "good" job. There's enormous freedom in this kind of detachment from ego. Ideas are able to more readily surface.

Choose a medium, the least threatening one, and play

with it. You can express current ideas through it or just see what comes to you. Have a good time with it and let your imagination roam where it will. Aside from being a free channel of expression, this exercise also enables you to work with those facets of a subject that don't typically arise, or haven't yet arisen, in your own medium. An artist wrote this poem:

Touching.
Touching a plane.
Springing from line.
Pulling and nodding.
Tension and pressure.
Curving in space, body in place.
Falling, the weight is falling.
Lifting, the colors rise.
Turning, the light is turning.
The red to dust, the black to dust.
Circular and perfect, the movement returning,
Like water changing and memory burning.

What started out as an exploration of the experience of painting evolved through the poem into a description of a painting. "I've never described or listed the elements of painting this way before. By making myself put into words what painting is, to me, I ended up describing things, ideas, that I had never envisioned before." This experience clarified some of the artist's goals that he had not been aware of.

You can get a similar freedom in your own medium by changing your customary methods or equipment. A sculptor commented, "Working with an unfamiliar tool or different materials enables me to just follow the directions the materials suggest. It keeps me from letting my preconceived ideas mold the piece. The pieces don't always come out nice and complete the way they do if they're intellectually planned, but I usually discover something totally new, some image or effect that I'd never imagined before."

And an actress began taking long nature walks and photographing what caught her eye. It helped her, she commented, to develop another avenue for her creativity and, even more important, to stick with her own vision. She was accustomed to asking others for their opinions about her work, and thereby diluted her own creativity.

3

CHILDHOOD: THIS IS WHERE IT BEGINS

Everyone has a child living within, sometimes a playful, carefree and loving child; other times a sad, lonely, unhappy child whose needs have not been truly met. Most of us ignore this child or are unaware of its existence. Our child is a valid part of ourselves that needs to be acknowledged, as well as a source of imagination, mystery, spontaneity, joy and, yes, pain. Occasionally I will meet a person who remarks, "I don't want to go back to my childhood, it was too painful. I want to forget it," or a person who will say "I had no childhood." But by burying this vital part of ourselves, we deprive ourselves of happiness and excitement; we perpetuate the dissatisfaction, detachment, or neurosis that may already exist. I wholeheartedly agree with Jeanne Segal, who in her book *Living Beyond Fear* says that avoidance is holding ourselves aloof from the raw material of our experience. She writes, "Only through opening to that pain can we find our vitality, our freedom to choose, our power to heal."[2]

Psychoanalysts have also recognized the correlation between childhood and creativity. Melanie Klein, a leading psychoanalytic theoretician, explains that creativity is a response to the unbearable pain of loss and separation that the child experiences in growing up. The most crucial experiences take place very early in life, usually beyond our recollection, and they give rise to intense feelings of guilt and anger toward the very person the child loves, which can lead to anguish and depression in the child. One of the most dramatic changes occurs at the age of about two and a half, when the child separates from the mother and begins to discover that he or she has a self. This is both exhilarating and frightening. Through art, says Klein, we repeople our world and re-create the self. In this way, we work through the depression of loss, according to Hanna Segal, another renowned psychoanalyst. And Fritz Perls, father of Gestalt psychotherapy, claims that by bringing forth our missing parts, we become whole again.

Bear in mind how many creative artists have recovered their childhood as the source of their work: Eugene O'Neill, for example, in *Long Day's Journey Into Night*, a play that reenacts intense familial conflicts, including his mother's addiction to morphine. Or Tennesse Williams' *Glass Menagerie*, the heroine of which, Laura, is based on Williams' beloved but mentally ill sister. Marcel Proust's series of eight allegorical novels, *Remembrance of Things Past*, is the outcome of an experience he had as an adult one day while eating a petite madeleine. The sensation of biting into this delicate little cake brought back childhood memories of Sunday mornings in Combray, France, with his Aunt Leonie, when they would dip the cakes into their tea. This memory led to a further train of associations and buried memories, and Proust locked himself in a padded room to recall and write about them. Eight volumes eventually resulted.

The re-creation of childhood is apparent not only in literature but in the visual arts and music as well. Edvard Munch watched his mother hemorrhage to death at the age of five, and as an adult he re-created this experience in his many paintings of death and dying: in his most famous painting, *The Scream*, the clouds are painted red, suggestive of the blood he witnessed. These memories filter not only into the content of the paintings but also into visual elements such as line, form, and texture, and therefore we are likely to overlook their connection to true-life experiences.

Childhood memories often are represented as musical elements in the works of composers. Gustav Mahler, for example, as a child once ran out into the street after watching his father violently beat his mother. He came face to face with a hurdy-gurdy player grinding out a popular Viennese air. The contrast and absurdity of these sequential events became fixed in Mahler's mind, and he frequently juxtaposed high tragedy with light comedy in his music.

Childhood memories are available to all of us and form the basis for much of our creativity. The exercises that follow provide a means of exploring the relationship between the "adult" us and the "child" us. As we draw upon a wider variety of inner resources in response to any given situation, a more complete self can be found.

Exercise 9:
DIALOGUE WITH THE CHILD IN YOU

Start out by having a written dialogue with your child-self. Remember, this is not you when you were a child, but rather is the child currently living within you. Begin by envisioning this child; don't force a picture, just concentrate on experiencing that part of yourself and let an image arise. Allow yourself to feel fully whatever emotions are stirred in you. When you are ready, ask the child a question, such as "Who are you?" or "Would you like to say something?" and let the conversation flow from there. Write whatever comes to mind, neither censoring yourself nor forcing a response. If the child says nothing, ask it something else or ask why it doesn't want to talk to you.

Talk to the child about the feelings that arise in you and listen to what it replies without judging or analyzing. Concentrate instead on what emotions it evokes. You may find that this child feels hurt or has a lot of anger toward you or others; after all, chances are it may have been ignored for many years. Don't run away or close off these feelings; go through them instead.

Have as many conversations as you need to become comfortable with this child; once it expresses all its pent-up feelings the two of you will be able to explore new ground together. Write these conversations in your journal in dialogue format, and draw any visual images that appear to you.

Then take this child out for a special treat. Ask it what it would like to do (within reason) and then do it. As always, be aware of your response to the child's request, but even if it's not your favorite activity, do it anyway. When you go out for this activity, it should just be you and the child. While you're doing it, keep the child active and alive in your mind; you are not alone but rather with this person.

When you get home, write the experience in your journal. Be open to all the feelings that arise in you and find a way to express and explore them fully.

A recently-divorced man whose feelings of separation and loneliness were dominating both his life and his career had this exchange with his child-self:

ME: Hello, little boy. Tell me about yourself.

CHILD: God, you're such a grown-up. So serious. First thing you want me to do is define myself. Definitions entail decisions, and limitations. Well, I don't want to make decisions and accept limitations, and I don't see why you're in such a hurry to.

ME: I just want to understand you, know you, that's all.

CHILD: What's so great about understanding? Do you have to "understand" a flower to like the smell? Did rainbows become prettier once you "understood" how they were made? Give me one good, practical reason why it's so important to know how rainbows are made. I don't ever want to know. There are so many things to do, ways to be, and you pick "understand," the most passive and boring of them all. And if you did understand me, then what?

ME: Don't you think we're getting off the point?

CHILD: There you go again. You and your narrow ideas of how things should be. What is the point, anyway? And are you the only one who decides what it is? That's pretty bossy. I think I should have equal say in the matter, and I say there shouldn't be a point. So there! What are you going to do about it.

ME: Why are you being so hostile?

CHILD: I'm being hostile! Look at you! You just march in, don't say a word about yourself or make yourself vulnerable, and want me to spill my guts immediately, and probably in five good sentences or less. And then you bitch because you've decided there's some sort of point or meaning to all this, and I'm not following your idea of what it is. You're bossy, and presumptuous and rude and worst of all, boring! And then you say I'm hostile. I may just be a little boy, but we're equals here.

ME: Okay, okay. Can we start over?

CHILD: We can, but why bother? You want to be perfect, that's all, and since you screwed up this round, you want to erase it. It has nothing to do with me. Well, too bad. We'll go on from here and you'll just have to accept that you're not perfect and that you botched up the beginning of this. You're still being so serious. So what if you botched things up? What is this thing about being perfect? That's so limiting. It always seems like perfect entails just one way of doing something, while imperfect allows for millions. And who decides what's perfect anyway? How can an imperfect person, especially one as imperfect as you, conceive of what's perfect?

ME: You certainly have a lot to say.

CHILD: That's 'cause I rarely get the chance to talk. We always do things your way; it really isn't fair. And I could just shake you sometimes. You're so silly, but it's not even a good kind of silly; it's a dumb kind, a waste of time and energy. Loosen up, lighten up. Stop being so narrow and filled with preconceptions.

ME: I don't think I'm really that narrow.

CHILD: Well, of course you don't. I bet you think you're as open as you can be. What you can't see is that you've made your conception of "can" about an inch wide.

ME: Why do you think that is?

CHILD: You've got your values and priorities all wrong. All this cerebral, mental stuff about being smart and understanding everything. You're so caught up in doing and seeing everything the smart way. You know what you should do? You should make yourself be dumb for a day. Not use your brain at all, but just totally rely on the other stuff and see what happens. You'd probably learn more being dumb than being smart.

ME: What's the other stuff I should use?

CHILD: And you think you're open? It sounds to me like you're already starting being dumb. What about emotions, instincts, impulses, memories, physical experiences?

ME: Oh, that stuff . . . You want me to give up the one thing I'm good at.

CHILD: Be adventurous. Maybe you'll be good at this other stuff. And anyway, despite all your efforts, you're not that good at the mental junk.

ME: You know, you're talking an awful lot about me, but still aren't saying a word about yourself.

CHILD: You dummy. You really aren't that good at the mental stuff. I'm everything that I'm telling you you're not. Otherwise, how would I know?

ME: So you think I should be like you.

CHILD: Of course not! What would I want with a clone of myself? We're talking about degrees here, something you've never been particularly good at. You're black and white, only two possibilities. I'm every conceivable shade of gray; and I'm saying that you could add a little gray, and a little bit of me, to your life without it killing you. It would probably improve things.

ME: So what should I do to lighten up and widen myself?

CHILD: Ask different questions.

ME: Huh?

CHILD: Your approach is all wrong. It comes out in your questions. "What should I do?" That implies there's one right thing you could do to make everything perfect. Wrong question. Wrong assumption. It has nothing to do with doing something. It has to do with different priorities, a different kind of thinking. And not just different for the sake of being different. Different because your goals are different. Right now, what is your goal other than being rich and famous?

ME: Well, this is embarrassing. But I want people to like me. I want to be funny. I want to be sought after.

CHILD: Why don't you make your goal to communicate to others. See how open that is. Not good or bad or what you should or shouldn't communicate. Just that: communicate with others. And instead of trying to understand that by defining it and limiting it, experience it instead and see how big you can make it. Expand the meaning of communication so that the definition of it could fill a whole dictionary. Instead of conjuring up good stories about yourself, focus your attention on other people and communicate with them, about anything and everything. Focus on the act of communicating more than what you're communicating.

ME: Hmm, that sounds like a good idea.

CHILD: There you go with your "good" again. It's an idea. I don't know whether it's a good one or not. Maybe it's a terrible idea. Who knows and who cares? It's just something to do. Like it, or hate it, or don't do either and just experience it, but don't evaluate it or try to understand it. Get out of your head. You can't reach anyone else if you're stuck in your head.

ME: Okay . . . not to change the subject now, but I want to take you some place special, fun. Where would you like to go?

CHILD: Why do you want to take me?

ME: It would be fun. And anyway, it's part of this exercise.

CHILD: At least the second answer is honest. Okay, but you have to let me be the boss.

ME: So go be the boss.

CHILD: I want to go to an amusement park and ride on all the rides, even the scary ones that make you nauseous.

ME: Okay, but could we please skip the ferris wheel where you go upside down?

CHILD: No, I don't want to skip anything. Nothing there is going to kill you so you can just put up with it. Let's go soon.

The man took his child to the amusement park and wrote this account of the trip:

> The experience opened up whole new levels
> of awareness and feeling in me, one of those

occasions where you're truly aware of how limited your knowledge is. It got me out of my sadness. I couldn't get over how real this child was. He looked like Huck Finn and had a very strong, separate personality. The trip was such a paradox. To the rest of the world I was a man alone, going on rides by myself and sometimes suddenly laughing out loud. An admittedly odd sight, I got the expected stares. But I felt that I was in the company of a precocious child.

My initial skepticism regarding the whole endeavor vanished as soon as I let my child emerge during the car trip there, and it was replaced by excitement. Once there we rode all the rides and gorged ourselves on junk food galore. It was great. I was continually surprised, and often touched, by his perceptions and responses; he was wonderfully fresh, open, and free from judgment. Not coincidentally, he was also happier and more relaxed than I. Where I grumbled and complained because of long lines and a closed ride, he took it all in stride; those were just two of the millions of components that made up our day at the park, so why focus on them? He saw so much potential for fun and adventure in what *was*, he couldn't bother being distracted by what *wasn't*. He chided me a few times for my attitude; he told me it was my own damn fault that I often felt deprived because I insisted on diminishing my experience of things by dissecting them into boring little bits and pieces. I stayed up late that night, mulling over what he told me; he forced me to confront some painful truths.

The man later wrote this follow-up entry in his journal:

Meeting my child opened up ways of perceiving that encompassed more than I ever dreamed possible. I followed his suggestion of being dumb for a day; it was great. I felt myself stretching creative muscles that I never knew existed—and feeling more pleasure than I had in a long time. I began to feel alive again. My initial reaction was to become that little boy, until I realized that this response was just another example of my eagerness to leap at the "right way." My child was indeed openness and freedom, perhaps even the epitome of pure imagination. But my daily life requires structure. I had to combine the two by utilizing my imagination in order to fashion my structure. This exercise enabled me to dramatically widen my scope of reference and discover new ways of being with others—and even more important, with myself. I still talk to my little boy, and he never fails to point out some wall I've put in my way.

A working mother who's new job was eating up most of her time and energy learned a lot just from writing this exchange with her child:

ME: Where are you? Where are you?

CHILD: I'm still here, hiding.

ME: Why are you hiding?

CHILD: I'm afraid to come out.

ME: Why are you afraid?

CHILD: Because I might do something foolish.

ME: God forbid.

CHILD: See, I told you.

ME: Look here, child. I need you.

CHILD: You do? What for?

ME: To make me laugh at all the nonsense I have to put up with.

CHILD: Aren't you happy?

ME: I'm usually too worried to be happy.

CHILD: I don't know if I believe you.

ME: You don't sound like a child, you sound like an adult. I feel so much responsibility and I'm angry about it.

CHILD: Let me stamp my foot for you. I'll scream and rant and rave.

ME: Thanks. I guess sometimes it feels good to be childish.

CHILD: Let's forget about all this reality. Want to play a game?

ME: Well, maybe. What kind?

CHILD: Make believe. Make believe you can have whatever you want and do whatever you want.

ME: That's difficult. Besides, I don't know what I want.

CHILD: Oh, lighten up already. You're becoming a pain in the ass.

ME: I want to have fun, I do. We're supposed to play now. I'm supposed to take you out.

CHILD: Yeah, like out of this office.

After reading this to the rest of the people in the workshop, she said, "I'm glad about my success, but I'm also angry . . . I pushed for years to get somewhere, and now here I am and do I want to be here? I want to be a kid again. I don't want to worry about all this." She made a concerted effort to restore more of a balance in her life and to devote more of her time to enjoyable activities. In a recent communication she wrote that she had managed to take a less demanding position, reduce her working hours to half, and enjoy more of the activities that gave her satisfaction and pleasure.

If you are one of the millions of misled people who has a tendency to believe you are not creative, that at best you are merely an observer of the creativity of others, the next exercise is for you. The assignment is to recall all the times in your life when you've been creative. Not only does this exercise work as a powerful reminder that you indeed have been creative in your life, but it sometimes points you in a new creative direction, based on the cues from the past. Sit down with your journal and a pen or pencil and do Exercise 10.

Exercise 10:
RECALL OUTSTANDING MOMENTS OF CREATIVITY IN YOUR LIFE

A secretary who had many interests but wasn't sure which one to pursue did this exercise. She showed talent in several areas but never developed her talent to the point where it made a difference in her life. She'd dabble in one area, then in the other, and never felt satisfied or motivated enough to continue. Then she did this exercise. She found a quiet spot, took a few deep breaths, and reflected on all the outstanding moments of creativity in her life. This is what happened.

I sang, "Take Me Out to the Ball Game," in front of the whole camp when I was four.

I had a small role in a play as a page when I was five. I shouted out my lines and the audience howled with laughter. I was surprised.

I loved to get up in front of audiences and "show off." During a ballet performance with children my age (five), I stepped out of line and went to the front of the stage, where I made funny faces and made the audience laugh.

I read a slapstick comedy I had written about my family to my second-grade class.

I stood up in front of my fifth-grade class to read a report and in the middle of it, the whole class, including the teacher, burst out laughing. I had totally forgotten that I had covered the back of the page of my report with cartoons of everyone in the class, teacher too.

The next year, I played the part of a scarecrow in a play and got a lot of laughs.

At 12, I began drawing pictures of famous movie stars. I'd get so absorbed in doing this, that my mother had to keep calling me to come to dinner.

I spent hours listening to records of show tunes and memorizing the words.

After that I didn't do much.

The woman was astonished to recall how much she had enjoyed getting up in front of audiences and amusing them when she was a child. She considered herself to be a shy person, and this glimpse into her former gregariousness was a revelation. She began to remember recent dreams of singing in front of people, and it really didn't matter that she was off-key. The exercise got her in touch with a deep wish that she felt embarrassed to admit. She wanted to sing in front of an audience and make people laugh—something she had done quite naturally as a child. Although she was self-conscious, she decided it was worth the risk to pursue the thing she enjoyed so much. She found a coach to train her. She began to display her natural humor with small groups of people, just as she had when she was a child. She even got her husband, who would come home bushed after a day at the office, to laugh. It put a lot more fun in both their lives.

Exercise 11:
LIST WHAT STIMULATES YOU; RE-CREATE THE SCENE

Since ideas develop in the unconscious, that's the first place to direct your attention in order to enhance your inspirational powers. Nurturing and nourishing your creativity can translate into better productivity and more innovative ideas.

First, list all the things that stimulate you creatively, no matter how strange or minor they may seem. Jules Pascin, a 20th century painter, depended upon the aroma of rotten apples to evoke his muse, and he kept them in his studio. Write down as many stimuli as you can, and don't censor yourself regarding what you think should or shouldn't excite you. Nature, sex, art are just a few of the many subjects that stimulate people. Some of your own responses may surprise you. Study your list and see which items you'd like to incorporate in your everyday life. Small things can make a big difference, and you can increase your creativity by filling your environment with stimuli.

A teacher discovered that going to the ballet or theatre stimulated her the most. She wrote:

> Experiencing that creativity enables me to cut off a hunk of it—swallow it, digest it, and allow my own creativity to feed on it. It's as if hearing an explicit statement of music, examining a portion of a magnificent painting, or reading a brilliant passage allows me to get a glimpse of the collective creative soul. Just experiencing it engenders my desire to create something of beauty, to get outside of myself momentarily in that higher plane where I am unaware of any stimuli from the external environment. Instead I am attuned to some special music inside of me. It is not the music of notes and keys; it is more the harmony in my soul, when all my senses are focused on conceiving, producing, and synthesizing senses, thoughts and feelings.

Once you've examined what turns you on creatively, recall an occasion when you were intensely inspired while immersed in whatever you were doing, and write the scene out in vivid, explicit detail. Delve as deeply as you can and let yourself go with it; you want to re-create those feelings to the greatest degree possible. Your unconscious is open to suggestion, and the connection between *feeling* inspired and actually *being* inspired can go both ways. You'll be amazed at how much influence you can have.

A painter triggered his creative energy through writing this account:

I'm in my studio, rooted in front of the canvas. All that exists are colors, fluid, emotion-filled colors, and the multi-rhythmed movements of my hand making shapes appear by magic. I'm totally absorbed, beyond concentration. The rest of the world has disappeared. All parts of my body not engaged in painting have disappeared. Hours and hours go by but I don't move from the spot. I catch myself holding my breath and have to remind myself to breathe. It's coming out exactly the way I want, even better than I expected. I'm flooded with ideas and all of them are wonderful. I don't even feel like I'm making decisions. I don't know where my ideas come from; it's as if some invisible giant has taken my hands in his and is making them do his bidding. I'm racing so fast I feel like I'm in another dimension, somewhere wonderful in the Twilight Zone.

He reads this account whenever his creative energy is low and says it pumps up his adrenals and gives him the burst of excitement he needs to get going. Teachers have written about moments when they have felt a strong communication with their students and have carried on a lively interchange; advertising executives have put down on paper the step-by-step process they go through when their minds are firing new ideas. Tennis players get back into that feverish excited pitch when they write down the words that describe the experience. And in every case, rereading these accounts helps to bring back the creative state of mind.

4

IT'S AS EASY AS CHILD'S PLAY

PLAY

Most of us take our creative activity very seriously; we refer to it as our "work" and often associate it with intense, sometimes painful, feelings. The desire for perfection and the fear of failure so prevalent among many creative people can be a major source of anxiety. So it might be initially surprising to mention "play" in conjunction with creativity. But if you think about it, you'll see that "play" appears in all sorts of creative endeavors. A musician "plays" an instrument; an actor "plays" a part; a playwright writes a "play." It's no accident or coincidence that this particular word is used.

Consider what is embodied in the word "play." It suggests a spontaneous, carefree, lighthearted approach, a lack of concern over perfection, and a willingness to explore and make mistakes. When a child plays with an object, he discovers its properties by examining it firsthand and seeing for himself what it will or won't do; he doesn't approach it with preconceived ideas of what it "should" be or how it "should" work. In his classic book *Escape From Freedom*, the psychologist Erich Fromm shocked many readers by writing that when a child disengages the wings of a butterfly it is not an act of sadism but rather a desire to see how it flies and what makes it live. Not only does much of the pleasure in creating stem from this kind of fresh, inquisitive, experimental attitude, but, ironically, it is also a productive way to tackle creative problems. A computer programmer commented, "Whenever I'm stuck, and working on something so tough that it feels like the mental equivalent of digging ditches in one-hundred-degree heat, I force myself to mentally shift gears and approach the situation with a light, playful attitude. I try to see how absurd and ridiculous I can make it, and not only does it become fun, but invariably the solution to my problem appears as well." Modern research is at last beginning to verify that positive feelings change the way we organize our thinking and that happiness expands and enriches our perceptions and associations.[3]

Play also involves our physical selves. As adults we tend to forget how much we use our bodies in creative expression: in playing the piano, for example, or sculpting, acting, dancing, and even painting. Movement helps to discharge feelings. And it is part of the sensual aspect of creativity—for example, in the application of paint to a canvas.

Play begins very early in a child's life, before the development of other forms of learning. It is not merely random or meaningless frivolity but is related to the development of cognition. According to Phyllis Greenacre, a renowned psychoanalyst in the area of creativity, this period of playfulness precedes the development of speech and appears in "the blowing of bubbles, the varied testing movements of the tongue, clucking noises, smacking of the lips, or imitations of the sounds of others, human and subhuman, or even sounds from inanimate sources." She claims that this repetition of sounds that first occurs in play indicates the existence of those early thought processes that later lead to more sophisticated language.[4]

As the child gets older he takes his play very seriously, becoming absorbed in it with enviable intensity and concentration. The result is that childhood play is hugely imaginative; indeed, Sigmund Freud believed that creativity began in childhood games and play. He compared a playing child to a creative writer, noting that both reorganized the materials around them in new, more meaningful and pleasurable ways in order to create their own worlds.

Play involves both the imaginative, sensory right brain as well as the cognitive, logical left brain. When the child becomes an adult, according to Freud, he substitutes daydreams and fantasy for play. It's true that daydreaming can be a temporary, pleasurable activity—and when employed consciously can lead to creativity. Play, on the other hand, offers long-lasting satisfaction: the emergence of our world of senses, feeling, imagination, and values in a form that can exist and be shared in the real world.

Creative artists paradoxically have approached their "work" through *play* since time immemorial, and their work reflects it: Prokofiev's music for the ballet *Peter and the Wolf*, for example; Alexander Calder's whimsical drawings, mobiles, and circuses in which he himself sometimes appeared as a clown; and Pablo Picasso's succession of painting styles that resulted from his insatiable wish to play. Play is an attitude, a point of view, that many artists possess, but it is not the domain of the artist alone. Playing with her computer, the office manager suddenly visualizes a way to save her company thousands of dollars; the housewife playfully approaches her husband, who's a stay-at-home "couch-potato," and all at once wins his consent to go on a vacation.

One goal of this book is to help you regain and develop your sense of play in relation to your work and your life. All of us are able to get in touch with the child inside who retains the ability to see humor and to play even in the midst of tragedy. Play is active, experimental, free from the restraints of man-made laws, and play is fun. It is the ideal way to explore your creativity. The exercises in this chapter will help you re-spark and enhance that wonderful ability, and you can approach the book's other exercises playfully as well.

HUMOR

Humor is a close ally of play and can be an integral part of our creativity. Humor taps our unconscious creative powers as nothing else can. As Freud pointed out, wit is similar to dreams in that both gratify wishes and express hidden feelings and truths that are socially unacceptable in their overt forms. Hostility, rebellion, and sexual exhibitionism, for example, are common themes of both jokes and dreams but are acted out in real life only at the risk of punishment. Dreams disguise these wishes with complex imagery; when you decode the imagery to reveal the hidden message (which Freud perceived as a forbidden wish), you free the energy that was contained in the image as well as the energy used to suppress the wish. In humor, Freud noted, laughter lifts the censorship. Humor, therefore, becomes a way to release antisocial feelings in an acceptable way. As with dreams that have been decoded, with humor the energy once used to repress these wishes is made free and available to be used for creative endeavors. Take the following example. The dreamer dreams she meets an attractive man but notices he is wearing falsies. The dream itself is funny, but it contains a more serious message underneath the bizarre imagery. The message it contains is that the woman keeps finding dishonesty in the men she meets, hence the "false front." Behind the humor of this dream is the woman's disillusionment with men and the sadness it engenders in her.

Humor conveys several messages simultaneously and can render certain topics more palatable. It provides enough detachment so that one is able to examine a controversial issue without too many personal, unpleasant feelings cropping up to obscure the point. Humor also actively involves its audience by engaging its mind, first eliciting its assumptions and then challenging them. Humor invokes an immediate, pleasurable response; people like to laugh. Laughter, in fact, is a creative tool. Research has proven that laughter enables us to see new relationships and find creative solutions to problems.[5]

Humor can additionally provide an essential contrast in a serious work of art; Tennessee Williams is just one of the many writers who often used humor for this effect, and the juxtaposition of humor with its opposite, pathos, intensifies each of these moods. Many things can be accomplished with humor that would not succeed otherwise.

Humor and play originate from identical patterns of thinking. This doesn't mean that play isn't serious. Indeed one of the significant characteristics of children at play is their total absorption in what they're doing; at that moment it is of all-consuming importance. Also, just because something is funny doesn't mean that it's not real or serious as well; after all, nothing is funnier than something that is inarguably true. It is the truth's relationship to an unexpected context, assumption, or consequence that makes it funny. Creating this kind of juxtaposition requires the same open, imaginative, nonlinear thought processes as does play.

Anique Taylor, a New York artist, poet, and performer, can express things that are serious through her guise as a clown. She loves children, really knows how to talk to them, and had once thought of being a child psychologist. As a clown she uses her humor to reach children. This is her most effective tool for communicating with them.

Humor employs paradoxes and opposites, the possibility of the impossible. This is a major principle behind physical slapstick comedy. In reality, being hit over the head with an oversized sledge hammer is no laughing matter; the victim is likely to die with a hideous smashed skull. But if the blow of the sledge hammer has the impact of a pillow it *is* funny because it's impossible; two conflicting realities are occupying the same time and place. The extreme hostility expressed is acceptable because its manifestation is completely harmless; thus the hostility simultaneously exists and doesn't exist.

In humor, sometimes one thing is said but the opposite is meant. The listener is led down the path of logic toward what seems to be a foregone conclusion but then ends up someplace radically different. The laughter comes from realizing how he got there.

The unexpected conclusion is often created through an

early type of thinking, which Freud called primary process. It is evident in infants and very young children; the thinking is instinctual and requires the immediate gratification of wishes. There are no boundaries of time or space, and opposites are interchangeable. Also, similar entities are perceived and responded to as if they were identical. To a young child, for example, all toys are his toys. A thing's characteristics are taken literally; someone named Mr. Green is expected to *be* green, and the evaluation of those characteristics is uninfluenced by the normal relative value ascribed to them. Categories are subject to the vagaries of the emotions. How can any of us re-create this type of thinking? Through free association. And why would we want to? The answer is simple: through free association we tap the unconscious. The unconscious has a power and an impact we can never achieve through logical thinking. The more we can draw upon our unconscious, the more vital will be our creativity.

Understanding how humor is made will help you to create it. Faulty logic is another type of thinking valuable in humor; it is logic based on false premises, or it is a line of thought that is logical yet implies that there are additional facts that would invalidate the assumption. In both cases the logic conveys the opposite.

The creative person employs faulty logic in such a way that it passes as logic for a moment or two. An audience laughs because it realizes it's been fooled, thus it must initially have believed the ruse.

Exercise 12:
TAP YOUR HUMOR

To better understand how you can use humor creatively, examine closely something you enjoy doing that you find particularly funny. It need not be as explicit as a joke or a cartoon; a witty exchange in a dramatic scene or a small detail of a painting offer the chance not only to explore the workings of the humor itself, but also its relationship to a larger, more serious whole. Sculptor Alexander Calder, for example, often employed humor by signing his name in the most unexpected and inappropriate place in the artwork, such as in a circle around a belly button.

First analyze the humorous bit; what makes it funny? What are the paradoxes? What is being said, and what is really meant? What is the feeling or desire being expressed? Is there an interaction between logic and faulty logic? Dissect the humor, both what is expressed and how it's expressed.

Now examine how the humor works in relation to the whole piece. What is its role? What effect does it have on the whole piece, and how are the other individual elements affected by it? What would the piece be like without it?

The next step is to use humor in your own work, or in your own life. Don't consciously strive for humorous imagery; free association, with its built-in lack of constraints, is the best method. Free association is allowing the mind to wander freely and associate without censorship to a word, image, or idea. Select an idea or emotion you want to express humorously and free associate to it, exploring all its facets. List everything you can; don't censor yourself, judge your ideas, or try to be funny. Concentrate instead on being as open and free as you can. Allow yourself to take risks and be outrageous. If you find a certain angle or perspective particularly amusing go further with it, see how far you can pursue it. If not, keep jumping around between different approaches. Twist words, juxtapose visual images, play and experiment with ideas until you've exhausted all the possibilities. Then look at what you've created. A humorous image may have emerged full-blown, or perhaps it's just suggested in part of another image. You may find that combining two or more ideas gives you the impact you want.

A junior copy writer, interested in dating several women at one time, chose to explore the idea by doing this exercise. This is what he wrote in his journal:

> The Problem with Dating Several People at the
> Same Time is Remembering . . .
> Each one's name
> Each one's nickname
> Each one's life story
> Which story goes with whom
> What stories you've told whom
> The names of each one's siblings
> The names of each one's pets
> Who's allergic to cats
> Who loves dogs
> Who has hay fever
> Who's diabetic
> Who hates stuffed animals
> The name and personality of each one's boss
> Where you went to dinner on your last date
> Who always orders the most expensive thing
>   on the menu
> Who hates sushi
> Who likes miniature golf

Who hates politics
Who has the jealous ex-boyfriend who's
   getting out of jail
Whose mother had the face lift
Where you left your traveling toothbrush
Whose underwear is under your bed
Who's on a diet
Who's a chocoholic
The details of each one's last relationship
What each one wants from a relationship
Who's in therapy
What kind of therapy each one is in
The name of each of their shrinks
Who sincerely enjoys watching football
Who despises television and anyone who watches it
Who likes to make love with the lights on
Who likes to make love with the lights off
Who means "yes" when she says "no"
Who means "no" when she says "no"
Who knows karate
Who loathes baby talk

The copy writer realized that what made this funny was the fact that all these qualifiers that supposedly make up a person's identity really have very little to do with the person and the experience of being close to her. Not only was this a revelation for his life, but it gave him the idea to write a comic short story about a forgetful Casanova who adores women but can never remember the anecdotes and information they tell him. Women love him despite this flaw because he makes them feel beautiful and important. His superlative aptitude for true intimacy and emotional closeness is the direct result of his inability (or perhaps unwillingness) to recall all the details and items that we call our identity. When he hopelessly falls in love with one woman and decides to devote all his energy to her and remember everything about her, he gets lost trying to respond to her identity and loses his connection with the deeper parts of her.

Humor is a wonderful creative tool, and the ability to make others laugh is a special gift. It's also an ideal way to ease the tension in a strained situation and to have a positive impact on others. You can learn to use it in your creative work to give it more impact, variety, and accessibility; and you can use it with a life problem to introduce a note of lightness and a fresh approach to what may seem to be an impasse.

The free association exercise can give you a concrete experience of the vast number of creative options available to you. You'll find it enormously beneficial to use this technique in order to create multiple answers and solutions for both your work and your life.

Exercise 13:
PLAY WITH YOUR FAVORITE CHILDHOOD TOY

For most of us, childhood was the time when our imaginations were the freest. We were able to travel between reality and make-believe with ease and were not slaves to judgment, preconceptions, and even knowledge. Recapturing the free imagination of childhood can lead to greater awareness, for things will be perceived as they truly are, no more nor less, instead of as we the adult mind "knows" or "thinks" they should be.

Toys are the physical, "real-world" elements that the child connects with in order to enact his fantasies and to test reality. Play is the connection between the real world and the child's fantasy world. According to the renowned psychoanalyst, D.W. Winnicott, playing with a piece of blanket, a teddy bear, a doll or toy is the infant's first creative act. And a toy is an especially pleasurable outlet for expressing the child's fantasies.

Many creative adults retain their fondness for toys and games and find them useful in their work. A writer for a Saturday morning cartoon show keeps every inch of his office crammed with toys; some are the characters of the show itself. Writer Ray Bradbury surrounds himself with books, toys, paintings and maps he's owned since the age of three. Because of his love of dinosaurs, he was commissioned to write the screen version of *Moby Dick* by John Huston, who also loved prehistoric creatures.

Childhood toys and play can inspire powerful creativity. A city administrator who is often bogged down with important decisions and long meetings finds relief and satisfaction in going home at night to play with her toy trains. It completely relaxes her and allows her subconscious mind to come up with solutions to problems she hasn't been able to solve at the office. Suddenly she'll jump up from her trains to write down the solution to a problem she's had at work. So although playing is for sheer enjoyment, it sometimes gets her back on track—no pun intended.

An artist who was deeply connected to his own sense of play and fantasy expressed it in a large painting of a giant-sized child lying on the floor; the child was creating his world out of a chess set of human figures. The artist had made the inanimate chess pieces look human, illustrating how inanimate objects may become projections of the child's inner world of fantasy. The artist also sculpted a horse out of wood, poised to gallop off but trapped to the floor on stationary wooden runners. The rocking horse, made to look like a live horse, is a poignant metaphor for high spirit that is grounded. Both works convey some of the powerful feelings of childhood.

For this exercise, recall a favorite toy from a time in your early life when you were still young enough that your imagination outweighed your logic. The toy should preferably be one that you can play with by yourself. Then go to a toy store and buy it or something similar. Take your time browsing through the toy store; looking at the toys can spark forgotten memories as well as re-create the excitement and magic of childhood.

Bring the toy home and re-create as closely as you can your childhood play environment. Where did you play? Outdoors, in your bedroom, in the living room? Was it morning, afternoon, or evening? Was the radio or television on? Did you play on the floor, on the sofa, in your bed? What clothes did you wear? What food did you have? Were there any significant odors such as cooking? Did you use any particular accessories or props when you played with this toy? Was the weather or temperature a factor? These and similar elements may have performed important subconscious roles in your childhood play. Identifying them not only enhances your experience of this exercise but can also improve your current creative process.

If your favorite childhood playtime was six-thirty in the morning, when you were plopped in front of the living room television watching cartoons and eating a peanut butter and jelly sandwich, you may discover that your imagination continues to be the freest in this particular setting. Never underestimate the power of props and other similar factors in creativity. When you've re-created the physical environment, play with the toy. Try to recall your old childhood fantasies, characters, and scenarios. Don't tense up or pressure yourself if it's initially hard to play

or if your mind goes blank. Don't try to think up something or do something "good;" let yourself drift and be
absurd and have fun. Concentrate totally on the play.
Don't analyze the experience as it unfolds or judge what
you do.

When you finish, write, draw, or paint your experience.
You need not be literal at all. If you already have a particular medium that you are working in, express the experience in your medium. Then, when you're in that initial
development stage with a new idea, try to re-create this
feeling. This same unrestricted imagination and lack of
judgment will aid you in getting the most out of the idea
before applying the requisite refinements and considerations of your craft. Additionally, it will help you in anything you do—from teaching to interior designing to
learning a new language or skill.

A young woman recalled that her first favorite toy was
a huge white teddy bear named Big Daddy. Every night
she went to sleep surrounded by Big Daddy and eight or
nine other stuffed animals and made up adventures involving them.

She decided to re-create this childhood experience. She
bought a big white teddy bear and borrowed a few stuffed
animals from a friend's daughter. Employing memory,
imagination, props, and special effects (including an audio
tape of her sister sucking her thumb), she duplicated a
night thirty years ago. Afterward, she wrote this account
in her journal:

> It's eight o'clock at night, and my flannel pa-
> jamas and socks feel just like Doctor Dentons. I
> brush my teeth fast and hop into bed, arranging
> Big Daddy and the other stuffed animals in their
> carefully selected positions. As always, the sheets
> are crisp and cool and stretched very tight, so

that I'm pressed into the bed. My mother teases me a little about all my animals as she tucks me in, then kisses me and my sister, turns off the light, and leaves. The room is dark, but the door is open a crack so that a sliver of hall light can act as a nightlight. My sister, sleepily sucking her thumb in the bed next to me, is part of another, far-away world. On the wall next to me are slanted, hard-edged lines of light from the window next to my sister's bed. Softer patterns of light on the ceiling and other wall suggest animals and foreign lands.

I'm warm and cozy and safe. At night, stuffed animals are effective armor against a rough real world. And most reassuring is Big Daddy's solid presence next to me; he can handle anything. Big Daddy's strength and invincible power come from his unerring wisdom; he's perfect, almost god-like . . . good qualities in a person designated to protect me.

Big Daddy, the other stuffed animals, and I live on a huge raft that has a covered sleeping area. We're on the ocean, rocking on the waves. Big Daddy teaches us to catch fish and we cook them for dinner. At night there are lots of stars in the sky and Big Daddy tells us stories before making us go to sleep.

We travel to an exotic island. We can pick our food off the trees and the weather is so beautiful that we don't have to wear clothes. Big Daddy teaches us all kinds of things, about nature and survival and life. It's better than school because everything he talks about is important.

Big Daddy tells me not to swim in the ocean. I love the ocean, am drawn to it by its vastness, beauty, and mystery. When I'm in the water I feel like I'm part of the intricate, busy world beneath its surface. I deliberately disobey Big Daddy and go swimming anyway. Big Daddy catches me in the water. I'm not surprised; I set it up that way so that he could rescue me in case it was dangerous for me to be in the water.

Big Daddy firmly pulls me out of the water. He doesn't yell, act like he hates me, or tell me I'm bad, but he's determined to make me understand that it is wrong to disobey him. He talks to me, solemnly and specifically, then spanks me. I cry, but I know exactly why it's happening and part of me believes that I deserve it. I don't doubt for a second that he loves me. I expected to be spanked for what I did, and deep down I am reassured that things are as they should be.

When he's finished I go off by myself to pout and reflect. It's comforting to know that he will always be there to enforce certain limits. At the same time, I know that I will continue to disobey him, break rules, challenge boundaries. It's as essential that I do this as it is that he try to control me. I feel that I have total freedom to experiment because his discipline makes me believe that he would be able to prevent me from getting seriously hurt.

This exercise proved to be revelatory for this woman. The conflict between freedom from limitations and the desire for safety and protection has been a central theme in every aspect of her life, but she was surprised to discover that her concern with this topic started in very early childhood. She was fascinated by Big Daddy's character, especially the way he handled her transgressions, and decided to call upon Big Daddy whenever she felt insecure or alone. By thinking of him, she found herself facing life's difficulties with more confidence and ease, and a lot less pain. She recently suffered the disappointment of a failed relationship. She comforted herself with the idea that Big Daddy was there to protect her and love her. And it helped prevent her from her usual pattern of blaming herself when things went wrong.

Play not only leads to insights, it is the first and purest expression of creativity. Through play, you can experience the thrill of novelty, and you can discover by trial and error. Play renders the mind free of conflict, fear, and attachment to outcomes. It facilitates stepping outside the immediate situation and becoming accessible to new ways of seeing. The best time to begin incorporating play into your life is now!

Now that you have explored methods to enhance your creativity consciously, let's delve into your unconscious resources.

PART TWO

Incubation

5

ASK YOUR DREAM THE VITAL QUESTION

A 20th-century painter, I. Rice Periera gave herself creative tasks before dozing off at night. She called upon her dreams to provide answers and would awaken before dawn to paint the ideas and subject matter of her dreams. One such dream brought about a major breakthrough in her work; it changed her entire use of light and space and led to a completely new philosophy of painting.

When we ask our dreams for answers, we open ourselves to the highest wisdom within us. Dreams speak the language of the unconscious. They are a direct line to our creative power. Unlike the conscious mind, dreams have no investment in concealing or distorting the truth. When you ask them a question in earnest, dreams respond like superhuman computers, pulling forth pertinent buried data from your memory bank and your collective unconscious as well.

Everything you have ever learned or experienced from the first moment of life, beginning in the birth canal, is recorded in your memory bank. That includes all sensations, perceptions, emotions, thoughts, and actions, many of them not consciously noted at the time of occurrence. Your unconscious knows everything about you, including all the painful truths you've had to bury in order to survive in the world.

If you could flip the channel into your personal unconscious, you might see dramas enacted that are projections of your unconscious conflicts. Or you might tap into your collective unconscious, the term Carl Jung coined to describe the entire history of the race imprinted within every living person; according to Jung, each of us contains in our collective unconscious all human experience from its inception. Thus you might witness heroes, historic figures, and peoples of ancient times populating the scenery as well as mythological and invented animals. You might find yourself on a street from Charles Dickens' *A Tale of Two Cities* or conversing with Julius Caesar about the affairs of state. You might even glimpse one of your past lives or tune into your own birth.

One explanation of how this phenomenon occurs is the DNA theory. DNA (deoxyribonucleic acid) is a molecule containing the genetic material of the cell. It determines our inherited characteristics that are passed down from generation to generation. It has passed through all forms of life since the beginning of time. And its memory bank, with the history of its particular evolution, resides in every cell of the human being.

Considering the wisdom that is contained within each of us, it is no coincidence that Einstein formulated his theory of relativity while he was dozing, or that Bertrand

Russell "slept on" a difficult mathematical or physics problem, and then awakened with the answer. Countless others have found the answers they were seeking in their dreams, and many of them made important contributions to civilization.

What are the questions waiting to be answered in you? Are they related to material that was stirred up by Exercise 1, "Where would you like to be six months from now?" Are they questions about work, creative projects, relationships, life directions, what is important or meaningful to you, what will give you fulfillment? You may discover more questions cropping up when you do the exercises in Chapter 7, "The Power of Fantasy," because fantasy puts you in touch with your deepest wishes.

Formulating the question itself is a creative act, because it helps you to focus on what's truly important. When you ask the right question, you set your creative juices in motion. The right question opens up a space for something to fill, and the unconscious is drawn into that space.

Exercise 14:
PREPARE AN IMPELLING QUESTION

If a question does not come to you spontaneously, it is imperative to thoughtfully conceive what you want to ask your dream. Above all, you must have a genuine wish to know the answer. A question in which ambivalence resides will get no cooperation from your unconscious. But if you ask a question that is candid and straightforward, the unconscious will elaborate upon and reorganize your conscious input with related data from your personal and collective memories, perceptions, and experiences. And a dream is born! If you're lucky, the dream will provide an answer that is to the point, an answer that is indisputable. On the other hand, the answer may be like the riddle of the Sphinx, and dreamwork techniques can help you decipher the meaning that lies hidden in the dream. Keep your question short and to the point.

Only you can know what you will discover if you ask your dream for the answer to a creative problem. Try it and see. The following are examples of what others discovered when they asked their dreams to respond to their questions.

Stan, a gifted young man, had worked at several different jobs and was highly competent in each, but he could not find his direction in life. He had the following dream after asking his unconscious what direction to take.

> I'm in a wheelchair, and I can't walk. My family is in the room with me. My legs are numb, and I don't want to feel dependent on anyone. I force myself to rise up on my hands and arms, which become filled with pain from supporting my whole torso. I cry out in pain and my family rushes to my assistance and tries to help me. I'm seated once again in the wheelchair, and I notice some feeling coming back into my legs. I'm able to rise up on my own two feet.

Through analyzing this dream, Stan discovered that he was very angry at his family for never paying attention to him, especially when he was feeling insecure or needy. He was now at the point in his life where he had many interests but no real inclination to work. He had been drifting from job to job. The dream revealed that he desperately needed the emotional support of his family. And this dependency made him furious at them, something he did not want to admit on a conscious level. But dreams don't lie, and this one confronted him with the truth of his situation. Incidentally, dreams will not bring up anything that we are not ready to handle; those that do are immediately forgotten.

The dream convinced Stan that until he got the support he needed, he would feel aimless. The dilemma was that he never could, nor ever would, ask his family for support. They never had given it to him, so why would he get it now? The dream haunted Stan until the following night when he tried the incubation exercise again. He said to his dream, "Where do I go from here?" He had another startling dream:

> I dream I am pregnant. I am gathering my things together in preparation for the event. I have to go to my previous job—a warehouse where I work as a furniture mover. There is large industrial machinery. I turn the truck around and drive it backwards into the garage. My girlfriend comes in through the side door, dressed in a man-tailored pin-striped suit. She asks me with concern: "How are you? Did you do your watercolors?"

Stan was bewildered by the reversal of gender roles in his dream: he, a man, is pregnant; his girlfriend, in a man-tailored suit, is the breadwinner. His pregnancy is a symbolic way of saying he is filled with ideas and creativity. And the dream also suggests the way to express them—through his watercolor paintings or drawings. His girlfriend, the provider in the dream, offers concern and encouragement, qualities he had hoped to get from his parents. The dream gives him good advice: get what you need from your girlfriend, it tells him, not from your parents. She is more than willing to give it.

It was not easy for Sara to leave a position of twenty years as a senior editor of a book publishing company, to do the thing she wanted to do most: write a novel. But that's exactly what this dreamer did. Making this choice involved anxiety and risk; not only did she have to figure out how to make a living, she would be giving up an important position that provided recognition and many other benefits. Besides, she had no guarantee that she would succeed. It took a full year to make this enormous step, and the night of her office farewell party, she asked her dream, "Did I make the right choice?" Usually questions that demand a yes or no answer are not effective. However, this dream was an exception. She dreamt:

> I'm standing outside a toystore at night. The toy store is closed. I look at a toy, and I tell myself, "If it starts to move, that's a good omen." The toy not only starts to move but it comes through the air and remains motionless in front of me, facing me. I consider this a good omen.

The next night she had another dream:

> I'm lying on my back in bed, looking up at the blue sky. Suddenly a patch of sky detaches itself and comes right through the closed window and into my chest.

"Both of these dreams," she said, "came at a time when I really needed them, when I was just getting involved in my own personal writing. I felt encouraged by them because I believed they were signs that there was something special about me and that I had something special to say."

The dreams did encourage her. Recently she completed a second draft of her novel, and a prestigious literary agent has asked to handle her book.

A college professor named Ted had serious differences with the chairman of his department about the way he wished to teach his class. Ted was not the type of person who would ever bend to others, and he insisted upon doing things his own way. So he asked his dream how he might resolve the dilemma. This was his dream:

I'm at a cocktail party. Everybody is drinking oversized cocktails with these little creatures in them—miniature creatures that look like furry brown Miss Piggys. It's all very trendy and they swallow the creatures like olives. These gerbil-like creatures are alive, but they die in the alcohol. And it's all very polite and posh and all that sort of stuff. I don't want to drink this thing so I stick it in my pocket while they're not looking. And I take it home. It communicates by telepathy. And so it thanks me for saving it from dying in the alcohol. I then feed it and don't say anything to my neighbors or anyone else about it. And it keeps growing and growing and growing until it's about the size of a saber-tooth tiger . . . and looks like one too. It's got these long curling tusks that look like ram horns. But it's very nice and unaggressive, just big and striped and it still looks like Miss Piggy with brown fur and big round amber eyes. And it still communicates by telepathy.

It becomes necessary to go out and save another one that this thing has communicated with by telepathy. It's hiding out, it's scared and we go and rescue it. It's hiding out in a back alley behind some garbage cans. Somehow we get it home and I now have two of them. And it's becoming progressively more difficult to keep them hidden. So the authorities come to check out rumors that I have these two things in my space. And the authorities are confronted by these two rather large and ominous-looking creatures and myself. We have to leave the city because there are no permits for having these things, and it's a criminal offense. So I find myself having to go out to the outback, which is a place outside the city where you don't have the so-called protection of civilization. So we leave, the creatures and me, to go into the unknown outback.

Ted is someone who cannot compromise his beliefs. He's an original thinker and has strong convictions. Admirable as this is, it makes his life difficult and he often feels like an outcast, which the dream clearly shows, because he refuses to play the game. However, he is a resourceful person, and the dream helped him to realize that he just is not happy in an environment where he must submit to the program of others. The dream got him to think about other options: consulting, writing full-time, lecturing as a guest speaker at other universities. He began forming scholarly groups with compatible peers, publishing academic papers and essays on topics that interested him, and getting his book accepted by a publisher. And although he was a tenured professor—a position few people would relinquish—he has just given notice to his university.

Unlike Ted's dream, which he clearly understood, some dreams confuse and elude us. For example, a playwright had a dream that both baffled and traumatized her. The dream took place in a setting familiar from her childhood, but that was all she could recall about it. She became totally blocked after the dream and felt that nothing she could do would unblock her. Before that she had been writing prolifically. Three weeks later she decided to go back to her dreams for an answer; she asked for another dream that would release her creativity from its bondage.

> I promised myself that I would be strong and remember the event that lead to this impasse. That night I had a dream which seemed to have no connection with what I had asked. But in this dream a building appeared where I had lived as a child. I don't remember exactly how it happened, but after the dream I recalled and experienced intensely some traumatic memories. I experienced it as strongly as if I were there at that moment. So I figured out that my first dream was telling me why I couldn't create, and the second dream enabled me to *feel*—not only understand, but *feel*—the fears I had as a child. And so the next day I was able to start writing again.
>
> In my second dream, several men come to my house and begin to move the furniture around as if they are preparing to take it away. They turn one table upside down, and I ask them where their license is to move furniture. They don't pay any attention to me. I try calling the police but can't get through to them.

The part of the dream when the men turn the table upside down brought back a childhood memory of her father overturning a table where she kept all her books. "My father was a brutal person; he didn't like me because I was too smart for him. He never let me talk or express myself. I hated him as a child. He would force me to do things in a brutal way. I had to sweep the kitchen floor and I hated doing it. One time he forced me to do it and I resisted. He put his hands around my throat, and I thought he was going to strangle me to death. It was this memory that I re-experienced, feeling all over again the same fright and humiliation I had felt as a child." The reliving of this experience freed her of her block and she's writing full-force again.

On a return trip from Italy another woman, June, had a portentous dream. Her mother had recently died. Exhausted from several months of caretaking and grieving, not to mention dealing with red tape and indifferent hospital employees, June wanted to get as far away from home as possible. Her boyfriend pleaded with her to join him on a trip to Italy. The public relations firm where she worked agreed to give her time off. Her employer had been supportive all through her mother's illness. On her return flight, however, June began to reflect on the changes her mother's death had made in her life; she started to question how she wanted to spend her next ten years. Her job was waiting for her, but she wasn't sure this was what she still wanted to do. She thought about her future on the plane, and as she was dozing off, asked her dream for direction.

Figures from a painting appeared in her dream and began moving around, making different configurations. They resembled the work of the futurist painter Fernand Léger, and it was the future she was concerned about. When June woke up, she felt excited and alive, sensations she had not experienced for several months. She realized that she wanted to paint. There was so much aliveness in these dream images and so much feeling—and she suspected many of the answers to her life were contained in those images. She had always loved art but as an observer, visiting museums and galleries and reading about art. She had never drawn, painted, or sculpted.

June figured out that she could support herself for two years on the modest inheritance that had been left her and decided that if, at the end of that time, she was not moving forward and enjoying painting, she could always return to work. She had excellent references and enough experience to easily get another job in a public relations firm. She left her job three weeks later.

Another dreamer, Susan, used to take the subway to work every morning with her sister. But one day she and her sister had a falling out, and they stopped speaking to one another. She didn't give it too much thought; one night, however, she asked her dream if she should reconnect with her sister. Her dream surprised her.

> I am in the subway. My sister is going to work; she's in the last car. I'm in another car on the same train. We stop for a light in the tunnel. Another train from behind crashes into our train, hitting the last car and crushing it. The people in my car are all thrown up against the poles, the doors, and the walls. Some fall on the floor. I remember that my sister is in the last car and I rush back to the last car and find that she is severely injured, that I have lost her. I start weeping hysterically, feeling the pain of the loss. I sit up in my bed (both in my dream and while awake) and I wake up.

As Susan was waking up, she reported, "I found myself sobbing uncontrollably. And I realized why I was crying —as I had never cried before in my life about anything. It was so deep. It was because I was grieving for the loss of my sister. I realized how much I loved her—which I really wasn't aware of before this dream. After the dream I began to appreciate her more, and to feel she was more dear to me now. I still didn't express this; she knew I was always there for her and that I loved her." Along with the recognition of this feeling of love, other things were released in her too. She once again began to do the things she had loved but had abandoned—her long walks in the woods, her ceramics. She felt a renewed enthusiasm for life.

Ellen, a young Ph.D. candidate in art, was putting herself through school, working part-time to support herself. She could not figure out why she was feeling so discontented. Her life seemed to be going smoothly. She asked her dream, "What's making me so discontented?" This dream followed:

> I am in a room. I look through a doorway into another room. The room I am in is filled with different colors; but the other room is black and white. A woman is in the room, also wearing black and white. I recognize her as my boss.

Ellen recognized the dream's message immediately. It was describing the way she perceived her boss saw everything: in terms of black and white. She herself saw many shades in between and felt many nuances; this was represented in the dream by the room in which she was standing, which contained all the colors people normally see. The dream helped her to understand why she was feeling stifled in this job—a feeling she had not been conscious of until she had the dream. She reflected on how excited she had been about this job when it had first been offered. She was to assist a museum curator, which would give her excellent experience in art, she thought. She had hoped she could learn on the job and contribute her ideas as well. Her boss originally had promised her a voice in the selection of artists, the writing of releases, and the hanging of art shows. But this boss, she soon realized, had no intention of including her in any of the decisions. The boss had one way of seeing everything and was not open to other opinions. She lacked imagination and good taste, to boot. The dream spelled out the problem so clearly that Ellen believed she had no recourse but to resign; the price was too high, she said. She had recently met an art historian who needed a researcher to gather material for the book he was writing. Their personalities had clicked, and the job was still open when Ellen called him. She was able to move from a black-and-white situation to a lively stimulating one, where her ideas would be listened to.

Since creativity often goes hand in hand with healing, the question you ask can apply to healing as well as creativity. Healing is a natural by-product of creativity. The arts are filled with examples of people who have worked through conflict and illness in the process of creating art, but it is not only in the arts that this occurs. Other forms of creative endeavors can have this result. One of the immediate benefits of creative activity is an increase in self-esteem. The act of creation, however, can accomplish much more than this; it can be a working through of conflict and pain. Both Leonardo da Vinci and Edvard Munch fended off and overcame psychosis through painting. The American painter Elizabeth Layton finally conquered a thirty-year bout with manic depression when she began drawing her self-portraits. She had received thirteen shock treatments, drug therapy, and psychotherapy during her illness, and nothing had worked. At the age of 68, she began to draw herself engaged in the basic scenes and conflicts of her life, such as running from male domination and grieving over a dead child. Her work progressed over a period of time from expressing anger, fear, and unrelatedness to expressing jubilation. The gradual restoration of her mental health can actually be seen in each of her portraits, until finally she stands triumphant, victorious over the illness that had destroyed most of her life. Not only did Elizabeth Layton regain her mental health, she also earned national recognition as a prominant artist.

Another artist, Nancy Freed, coped with the horror of her mastectomy by making sculptures that depicted her feelings, such as screaming faces and a figure holding a breast in one hand. Through her sculpture she worked through her feelings of terror and loss. She went through several of the stages that Elizabeth Kübler-Ross outlines in her book *On Death and Dying*: the anger, the depression, and finally the acceptance. Not only was her work healing for her, it also offered viewers who had had a similar experience the comfort and relief of openly coming to terms with their own overwhelming feelings.

Scientist-philosopher Buckminster Fuller was a step away from death when he invented the geodesic dome. He had come to the end of his rope; he had lost his job and his wife wanted a divorce. He went to the water's edge to drown himself, and as he was about to end his life, the structure of the geodesic dome came to him as if in a vision. He forgot all about suicide, rose from the scene with a mission in mind, and proceeded to work on building his invention.

Freud believed that through creativity the neurotic person could find his way back to reality. Fritz Perls, the father of Gestalt psychotherapy, insisted that all of us are born with an urge to restore order. It is the creative artist who restructures the deficient patterns.

Several people in my creativity workshops report healing dreams when they do the incubation method. Bob, a college student, developed a physical condition that shocked and frightened him. He discovered boils on the inner thigh of one leg. After the boils had been there for a few weeks he finally called his father, a doctor, for a diagnosis. His father had told him not to be alarmed. As Bob drifted off to sleep, he kept repeating the question until he fell asleep: "What is causing my boils?" This was his dream:

> I inspect the largest boil on my inner thigh. It is about ten inches in circumference. It turns into a three-dimensional sphere no longer attached to my leg. There is an axis through the center of the sphere which sends out radiating light and energy. As I am looking at this sphere, I think of having sex with my mother. I go into a trance. My eyes roll back into my head and flicker. I feel very tightly held together, constricted. There is a lot of force in my head and pressure in my gut.

When Bob woke up, the boils had miraculously disappeared. "It is as if a huge weight has lifted from my shoulders," he said.

> I was shocked at the message of the dream but I knew the dream was telling me something important. I knew I needed professional help to understand what was going on. Once I made the decision to go into therapy, I no longer felt so helpless. I wanted to deal with my emotional problems directly and not develop physical symptoms instead. I developed the boils at a time when I was graduating and couldn't write my papers. And this seemed to disappear too when I had the dream. I was able to complete my

course work, and I graduated in June. I know I
was going through a real crisis, and am only now
beginning to understand the implications of it.

Another woman had a healing dream when she asked
for comfort and support from her dream. She was dis-
traught over her father's imminent death. That night she
dreamt she was taking care of a translucent white baby
made of light. There was a man wearing a plaid shirt who
looked like Jean-Paul Belmondo, the actor. He reminded
her of her handsome father, who also looked like an actor.
She recognized that the translucent white baby was an
image of spirit, which gave her great comfort during this
period of distress and grief.

A problem people frequently report as an obstacle to
their creativity is lack of time. Sometimes lack of time is
merely an excuse; at other times it is a reality. Cynthia
learned an important lesson when she asked her dream
how she could ever find enough time to complete her art
project. She had been trying to escape from the pain of a
recent divorce by making herself very busy. She was determined to avoid all those "bad" feelings—sadness, anger, depression, loneliness, feelings of failure—so she
threw herself into a maelstrom of activity. She made herself busy every evening and throughout most of the day
too. She arranged to be away every weekend, visiting
relatives, seeing friends, taking trips out of the country.
She bought tickets to concerts and the theatre, threw dinner parties, did volunteer work once a week with disabled
children. She attended lectures. She made up her mind
to live *now*, and recklessly spent money in the process.
She arranged to add a garage to her country home, replace
all the old windows of her house with maintenance-free
aluminum, renovate a bathroom. She even made the decision to finally confront her daughter, who had been

borrowing large sums of money from her for several years and refusing to work or pay her back. Cynthia was feeling exploited and knew that in the end she was hurting her daughter by giving in to her wishes. But she always found it difficult to say "no" when her daughter requested money. So she decided to bite the bullet and have it out once and for all with this misguided child. She knew she'd be barraged with screaming protests and hateful attacks.

The oddest thing of all about what was occurring was that Cynthia had set aside the activity that mattered the most to her. She was scheduled to exhibit her work at a respected art gallery in just two months, but had totally stopped painting in order to participate in these other activities. She got a call from the gallery owner one day, and this suddenly jolted her back into reality. She panicked. How could she ever complete the paintings in time for the exhibition? She had left no room in her schedule to paint. That night as she was dozing off, she asked her dream, "How can I complete the paintings in time for my exhibition?" This was her dream:

> I am in a field, lying on the ground. The breeze is softly caressing my hair. I haven't a worry in the world. It reminds me of a Van Gogh field of wheat. I notice three easels in a semicircle around me. On each is a blank canvas. As I am staring at the one directly to my right, I see the blankness has taken form; it's a painting of a figure running through time. I look at the second canvas, and cannot make anything out although some forms and shapes faintly appear. It looks disjointed, it doesn't hold together. A group of people stand around it, and a voice says, "C.A. is second-rate." [C.A. are her initials.] My attention is magnetically drawn to the third canvas,

even though it still remains blank. And I am now standing before it with a paint brush in my hand; the brush is dripping with thick oil paint. My hand moves the brush up to the canvas. It moves as if directed by an outside force. I am not in charge but witness this happening to me. Embryonic forms appear in deep greens and browns. I am revolted yet fascinated by the forms that emerge. They move upward to the top of the canvas, resembling lush overgrown vegetation.

Cynthia awakened from the dream with a feeling she hadn't experienced in a long time. "It was the same feeling I've had in the past when I was immersed in my painting and nothing else. And the thought that came to me was 'Immerse yourself in your painting and nothing else.'"

Suddenly everything fell into place. She decided to call off or delay all the plans she had made. The exhibition would be her priority; everything else could wait. This involved calling people and changing plans, something she hated doing. But she was making herself free for nothing but her painting. And she made up her mind to confront her daughter—*after* the exhibition. She also arranged to build the garage, replace the windows, and renovate the bathroom—all *after* the exhibition. Her decision to put everything else on hold was a conscious one that flowed naturally out of the message in her dream. And once she focused on her painting, she needed no outside distractions. The creative process offered her exciting rewards; painting became her constant companion, one that would not disappoint her as other "companions" had in the past. It restored her interest in life in a way that no other activity could. Nothing replenished or absorbed her more than her own creativity. She realized she had been looking for satisfaction in the wrong places.

If you are putting off your creativity because of time, you can learn from this woman's experience. Usually it is a question of your priorities and what you deem to be most important.

Summoning forth your unconscious through a dream is an excellent habit to cultivate. It can contribute to a connection with the unconscious that proliferates in time. Like a river, the unconscious unearths treasures as it continues on its course. When you flow with the creative process, your life also becomes a source of surprises and rewards.

6

IN DREAM-LIKE STATES

One way to tap your creativity is to do what the artists do. Many artists put themselves into a trance-like state of mind when they create. They are, in effect, suspending the conscious mind to enable the unconscious to filter through and actually take over. Then it is as if a painting paints itself, a poem writes itself, a garden plants itself. This is a very desirable way to work because it's unpredictable, it's fun, it's engrossing, and it puts us in touch with the deepest and most imaginative part of ourselves. When artists are in that state, they claim to lose themselves, to forget what time it is. They may suddenly realize it's four in the morning and they have been working nine hours straight. Nevertheless, this is a frame of mind the creative person desires. What a relief to have the critical mind suspended, not controlling one's life.

You may recall from Chapter Two, "What Stands in Your Way," that judgments and concerns over perfection are major obstacles to creativity. Chapter Six, in effect, provides an antidote for that problem. When a person creates in a dream-like state, the critical mind still exists but does not control. It is as if the unconscious is the horse and the conscious is the rider. The rider can keep the horse on course, gently steering it to the right or left, and preventing the horse from going wild. But the horse is the driving force and the magic. When you get in touch with this state of mind, it does not matter what form your creativity takes. This is a state of mind in which you're connected to your aliveness and your imagination. It can be used for whatever creative purpose you wish.

Dream-like states resemble, but are less intense than, dreams, and like dreams they tend to generate significant imagery from the unconscious mind. One artist who works in a dream-like state is symbolist painter Avel de Knight. Many of the symbols he uses, such as the pyramid, wings emanating from the head, spheres, and winged horses, appear again and again in his work. He purposely avoids knowing the meaning of these symbols, because cerebration can interfere with his inner process.

A poet who sometimes writes in a dream-like state is Judith Berke. She wrote this poem during such a state:

Echo

The woman entered the cavern
alone, except for a candle.
"Can't you see who I am?"
she asked (as if anyone cared)

but I sent her back
See who I am,
and *I am,*
and then she felt better.

What do you want of me?
I asked the river (cavern
river, motionless
river) and in it was a woman—
her body heavy
from swallowing all the words.

What do you want?
I asked, and no one had spoken first!

I don't want to see any more,
I said meaning the images
words make—*I/you, we/they,*
if we are we, then you
are nobody,
and knew then there was something besides
the words: so quiet, a sadness so deep

It was no longer sad,
and I stood up,
and went up out of that cavern into the open.

There is an imagery and emotional current in this poem that would be difficult, if not impossible, to duplicate in the conscious mind.

Not only can dream-like states free you, they allow more of your originality to surface. And the process is more engaging, more satisfying. The results of my own experience with a dream-like state actually turned out to be quite amusing, if not startling. I was making a collage out of fabrics. I began in the early evening, rummaging through my rags, getting more and more engrossed in what I was doing. But I couldn't find quite what I needed. I kept working well into the night, looking through drawers and closets for scraps of material that would give me the colors and textures I wanted. The next morning I was stunned by what I saw. There in my collage was a perfectly good nightgown that I had cut up into various shapes and pasted into my collage without giving it a second thought. I couldn't believe that *I* had done that. Where was I? It took a little time for me to adjust to the fact that I had lost my nightgown in the strangest of ways. But I did like the result. After all, I philosophized, what's a nightgown in comparison to a work of art?

Many people fall into dream-like states when they are walking, driving, sailing, floating on water, or engaged in some other lulling activity. These states often seem to be connected with motion. At those times, new ideas are generated, solutions are found. By not remaining stationary, we seem to let go of conscious thinking and allow a deeper, wiser part of ourselves to come forth.

There are various ways to induce these dream-like states. Suppose we examine one that involves motion that is not of a physical variety. Music evokes an inner emotional motion. It's interesting that the word "emotion" contains the word "motion" in it. Listening to music in a certain way can bring about the result we desire.

Exercise 15:
LISTEN TO DIFFERENT KINDS OF
MUSIC; WRITE OR DRAW IMAGES
THAT COME TO YOUR MIND

This exercise will elude your judgmental barriers. It combines three different steps for maximum stimulation and channels for expression.

First, listen to some music. Select a song, etude, symphony, whatever exemplifies your mood, or choose music you find provocative or energizing.

Then draw the first strong image that comes to your mind. It can be lines, a shape, a figure, or a scene. Allow the image to change and evolve as you draw it. Don't criticize what you do or try to make it perfect. Go for the feeling and keep it spontaneous.

Finally, free associate to what you have drawn. It can be a description, a response, a story, a series of images, feelings, or memories. Follow any new directions that present themselves. Then examine how you can use what you've done, in your life or in your particular area of creativity.

A woman who yearned to make a major and unexpected change in her life chose the song "I Got a New Attitude" by Patti LaBelle. The song exemplified the mood and theme she wanted her life to have. While listening to it she drew the figure of a buxom, self-confident woman, shoulders back, raring to go, and wearing a huge, elaborately beaded and feathered hat. Out of her free association came personality traits she had once shown, but later inhibited, and memories she had forgotten. She recognized in herself a flamboyancy that she had long buried, in her efforts to be the "lady" her parents approved of, self-effacing and sacrificing. She realized that this facade, this disguise of her true nature, was antithetical to her life. She decided that a "new attitude" was exactly what she needed.

Another woman listened to Stravinsky's "Valse Triste" and drew figures carrying musical instruments. The following free association to these images led to an unresolved childhood memory:

> I hear the wind, icy, coming around the mountain when she comes. The harp sounds celestial; they are celestial beings, angels, no doubt. And then a soldier with a French horn. A toy drum in Christmas green and red. The black drumstick threatens the drumhead. I remember something, a childhood incident I have always felt badly about. I broke my brother's Christmas drum. Interestingly, the red and green Christmas association came before the memory. I broke my brother's toy drum one Christmas morning by playing it too hard; I broke his chance for pleasure. And I didn't have the courage to tell my parents that I did it. And he was much too young to be able to say that it was broken, so he never got his big toy.

She then drew the broken drum, the bewildered, disappointed face of her little brother, and her own guilty scared expression. She knew she could never erase the impact the experience must have had on her little brother, a man now. She thought, "How can I ever make amends for this?" She and her brother were not close; they saw each other occasionally on holidays. She sensed her brother still looked up to her as his big sister, even though he had a family of his own. It was she who kept the distance, often making excuses that she was too busy to visit. In her wish to mend the past she decided to give her brother's two-year-old son a toy drum for Christmas the following year. This helped her alleviate her guilt and also establish closer ties to her brother; this was her gift to him and to herself.

A young executive listened to a song called "Nervous" by Mel Waldron. While listening to it he realized this song represented his creative self: "high energy, motivated, syncopated. Hitting certain notes hard and always moving. The music," he wrote, "was cat-like, stealthy, intricate puzzles suddenly popping up from an unexpected corner. A little danger—where will it lead. Such a euphoric, pulsating, captivating rush; it takes me over completely."

After doing this exercise, he made up his mind to listen to this song every morning to get his creative juices flowing. He could feel the rising tempo and pitch building in him. Concentrating on, following closely, the intricate melody line increased his concentration and focus, got his mind alert, moving. The melody, he said, "suddenly goes somewhere unexpected without losing the rhythm. That's the essence of creativity—going someplace unexpected without losing the rhythm—the vision, the integrity of the piece. Concentrating totally on the music gets my mind moving fast, free and limber to go in new directions." In the competitive field he's in, creativity stands high on the list for success.

A writer listened to the song, "It Doesn't Matter Anymore" by Linda Ronstadt. She became aware of the mixed message. The lyrics are the words of a strong woman who no longer loves her ex-lover, has totally gotten over him. But the melody and voice make it clear that that's a lie, and the bravado of the words only underscores the pain, make it seem stronger. "This is important in my writing,"

she commented, "to show characters expressing the opposite of their feelings, not coming straight on with them.
There are no pure feelings in good drama." As a result of
this exercise, she came up with a new exercise when
working on important scenes: namely, to have the characters say the opposite of what they mean and yet still
convey their true feelings through their actions. It's a way
to explore how they hide their feelings, she says, and is
an invaluable exercise she frequently uses.

Exercise 16:
STREAM OF CONSCIOUSNESS WRITING UPON AWAKENING

James Joyce, William Faulkner, and Virginia Woolf were
pioneers of the method known as stream-of-consciousness
writing. It came at that time in history when Freud
was having a tremendous impact upon the world, and
writers, artists, and others were hungry to experiment
with new methods. The idea of tapping the unconscious
was new and exciting. Even though these methods of self-
expression may seem passé today, stream-of-consciousness
writing is nevertheless an excellent tool for bringing forth
the unconscious. Freud introduced the method of free
association in his work with patients in order to catch
them off guard and allow the unconscious to break
through their defenses.

When you combine stream-of-consciousness writing
with waking up first thing in the morning, you are dou-
bling your chance of tapping the unconscious. It is during
the early morning hours that you have your longest and
most vivid dreams. You are still close to the dream state

when you awaken. Having a pad and pencil by your bedside works well not only with recording dreams but also with doing stream-of-consciousness writing. The purpose of this exercise is not to increase your skills as a writer, although that may be a secondary benefit, but to tap the creativity that lies within. Be sure nothing will disturb you—people, pets, ringing telephones—for the next twenty to thirty minutes. Write down all the thoughts that come into your mind without censoring any of them. Even if you have thoughts such as "I have nothing to write," write that too. Simply write them down, and then continue with the next thought.

A woman who could not break through to her creativity but knew it was there wrote the following:

A dinosaur's gentle direction could be any way. It could be down, it could be up. What a nice gentle face. I link the word "dinosaur" to "whoa mother."

Stopping after a fast run, so gentle, so sweet. Strong yet gentle in his direction. Stop awhile. Still, the power is there. And there's another one, a little menacing. And gosh, a gash on the back.

Sometimes it's just words. Sometimes it's just sounds. Sometimes it hits the mark. It has stopped. What hell, preacher, glorious keeps honest. Yes, the words can misguide.

Can I love this animal? And boats and fire at the back. Ironic too. No, there's the gentle, sensible one. And there's the menacing force disguised as another one. Admirable dinosaur. But what arrow? Is it your face, a female preacher that will eventually die? See? Belly on the land, just to rest.

Writing this, the woman said, was very helpful. It made her aware that her twin sister has always been a force keeping her back . . . though she did admit that she too stood in her own way. "My sister keeps me back because of a certain quality that she has that I don't have. I read that into the two faces of the dinosaur . . . However, I hold back my strength and that's what's stopping me from expressing my creativity . . . you know, the gentle dinosaur. Also the fear of going down. In this exercise I wasn't forcing myself to reach some kind of standard, and that wish for perfection is a tremendous block for me." This awareness brought her a step closer to freedom and self-expression.

Tim, a man who was having a streak of bad luck in his life, did this exercise when he woke up one morning. The public relations firm where he worked was rejecting his ideas. He was also having financial problems and was fighting all the time with his wife. Before brushing his teeth or even having his coffee that day, he immediately grabbed the pad and pen on his night table, positioned there for inspirational flashes should they occur, and scribbled away.

What to write, what to write? My mind is blank, blank, blank but I must keep going. Did William Faulkner and James Joyce do stream-of-consciousness this way, did they feel this? I hate this. What pressure! Who cares that it doesn't matter whether it's good or bad; it's hard enough to keep on thinking nonstop. Maybe if I get bored of writing garbage, maybe if I break through this, a gem will come out of me from being irritated this way, the way an oyster makes a pearl. That would be nice, lucky too.

Do I feel that lucky today? I don't know. Probably not. Doubt, doubt, doubt. Why is it easier to be negative than positive? If you think about it, the odds are probably even that it could turn out either way, so why do I always seem to bet on the negative, why does that seem more likely? My experience, I guess. I bet not everyone feels that way. I bet there are a few people who are lucky with the dice, who feel confident that things will turn out right for them, as if it's their birthright, as if they not only deserve it but are assured of getting what they deserve. I'm not sure what I deserve, but I don't feel any connection between what I deserve and what I get anyway. There's nothing to measure yourself against, that's why it's so hard. How do you choose your standards? And, having chosen, what should you receive for having chosen high ones? And how well do you have to fulfill these standards, and for how long, before you start reaping some benefits?

Maybe there is no connection. That often seems true. Despite all the preachy songs and sayings, maybe you don't really get what you give. Maybe they operate totally independently of each other, and there's no cause and effect at all. Or maybe it's giving in an entirely different way. Suppose someone discovered that your luck in life was determined by how often you wiped your feet before entering a house, or how many raindrops have fallen on the left side of your head. Imagine discovering there was a direct correlation between something arbitrary like raindrops and your quality of life. You'd have to stumble upon it accidentally, because there's certainly no way our logical brains would relate the two.

The chances of learning something like that are probably one in three trillion, but suppose it happened. What would you do? Would you tell other people? Probably not, you'd want to explore it more before telling anyone, even your closest friend, though it would be hard to keep your mouth shut. I mean, you would have discovered the meaning of life! You'd probably go around with a huge smug smile on your face, and move up to Oregon or some other rainy place and walk around with your head cocked to one side. And all kinds of issues and questions would come up. How would you know when enough raindrops had fallen on your head? You could spend half of your life collecting good luck and then, when you set off to materialize this good luck, die of pneumonia or something. Could you share this knowledge? Ultimately, I guess it comes down to: is there finite or infinite good luck? It seems to me that good luck can be infinite but that raindrops, in a given period of time, are finite.

Having written this he found himself feeling more optimistic about life, deciding he would go through the day believing he had the gift of good luck. And when he did this, his luck began to change.

A writer did this exercise with the intention of thinking up new ideas for articles; two hours and eleven typed pages later, he had four separate, viable concepts. He now uses this exercise regularly and says he never fails to get something he can use.

Exercise 17:
THE FLOWER EXERCISE

When your inspiration is at a low ebb and you feel there is no reason to continue on the creative path, try the flower exercise. This exercise offers more insights than perhaps any other. It also opens up your visual imagination and makes you aware of the awesome beauty that is uncovered when you allow yourself to truly look. The preliminary part of the exercise is enjoyable: go to the florist and select a flower that truly interests you. Take it home, put it in water in a vase, of course, and when you are ready, put the vase in front of you on a table. Allow yourself at least a half-hour of undisturbed time when you can sit and not worry about obligations or other concerns.

Have a timer by your side which you can set for ten to fifteen minutes. Take a couple of deep breaths and allow yourself to completely relax. Then look at the flower. Concentrate on its size, weight, color, textures; see the drops of moisture on the petals and stem. Look at the flower, in a relaxed contemplative way, until the timer buzzes. Then set the timer again, this time for five minutes. Close your eyes and let images pass through your mind without judging or trying to change them. When the buzz tells you your time is up, write in your journal what you saw, felt and thought during the five minutes when your eyes were closed. A woman contemplating a red rose had this experience:

> At first I pictured a mouth chomping at me several times as if it were barking at me, trying to frighten me or shut me up. That's how I felt taken aback. Then I pictured being a little person

inside the flower, and I walked among the tall stamens. When I walked, pollen showered down on me like rain. I was enjoying it but then I slipped down the stem of it, caught myself and climbed back up. I rested, panting, relieved in the comforting palm of the petal, where the petal meets the stem in a kind of cup. I was sitting there, held there by the petal, the petal supporting my light weight. And then I noticed rowdy kids yelling and screaming with the light, and they slid down another petal into the pistil field, and got showered with pollen. They were having fun.

I was frightened. I didn't want to try it. I was recovering from the near accident. But then I got the feeling I wanted to try. I got up and slowly made my way to the field of pistils and stamens, holding on to those tall stalks, and got covered with pollen, and climbed the chain of little people's backs to the top of the petal and slid down and heard them cheer. And better than their cheers was the joy I felt inside. A bubble of joy. I wanted to try it again, and this time I was more confident and quickly climbed up on the chain of people and slid down faster into the field of pistils. And the pollen showered down. I could do this again and again, getting more enjoyment each time.

This woman had long forgotten that she had such a playful, imaginative side. She had become bogged down in the pressures of her job and trying to support herself. She also discovered that, after her initial fear, she would take a risk despite her fear, and that the pleasurable results were well worth all the preliminary anxiety. One evening soon after, she took the leap and read one of her poems in front of a group of contemporary poets.

Another woman had a vastly different experience. She wrote:

> I felt very desolate after I closed my eyes during the flower exercise, after looking at the flower. And I couldn't see anything. It was more than a feeling of my eyes being closed. Everything went blank. And I missed the flower. It was the image of missing the flower. Later that night I had a nightmare in response to the exercise. My nightmare had to do with undergoing surgery. After this dream I was thinking about the actual experience of going under anesthesia, and the blanking out—just not remembering anything. So I wondered if the blanking out feeling when I closed my eyes had something to do with that. I was thinking also that the flower represented several people in my life who I have lost or I'm afraid of losing. So I wondered when I shut my eyes whether that feeling of desolation, missing the flower which represents these people, was activated. I had thought of this dream in terms of surgery; I hadn't thought of it in terms of loss . . . It was a powerful dream. It made me aware that I needed to reach out to people as a way to overcome my desolation.

And so she did. She began to share her more personal thoughts and feelings with others, and in that way, felt much less alone and sad.

A Sunday painter was having a painting block and reported: "The yellow in that iris kept bringing me back to some watercolors I had seen by Emile Nolde. What happened was I started seeing myself working with water-colors on Oriental paper. . . . I wasn't really thinking of my work at all; and all of a sudden that color just triggered all these realizations that I really want to start working again."

The last illustration is a metaphysical one:

> It's an African daisy. Where does the fragrance come from? The petals are so fragile. If you hold one between your fingers it soon turns brown at that spot. The flower will die soon. The flower can be so easily crushed and destroyed. Yet I feel the life force that moves through it. It comes from something that will go on and on, after my own lifetime. Nothing can stop it. It's like a Tai Chi master who never winces from the blow, because he hasn't resisted it. The flower is a paradox: superficially so easily blemished, so delicate, but inside stronger than steel, imperishable. The life force can never be destroyed. I feel it coming up from the roots of the world. I am the flower.

This was a very strengthening message for Maggie whose marriage had just fallen apart and who was feeling emptiness and desolation. It was a metaphor of faith, encouraging her to make something of her life. As you can see, people's experiences are vastly different, because the unconscious is vast and infinite.

7

THE POWER OF FANTASY

Fantasy is our unique capacity to give ourselves, through our imagination, everything we desire that is missing from our lives—and in the exact way that we desire it. Fantasies are among the most original expressions of our imaginations; nothing else creates, with such exquisite perfection, the precise situations that can satisfy our cravings and gratify our unfulfilled wishes. Fantasies can take the form of our personal pinnacle of success, the ideal encounter with a special person, the sight of ourselves at our glory, and even the perfect revenge. There is a Walter Mitty inside of each of us, but many of us are ashamed of this part of ourselves and undermine our fantasy life. Creative people, however, allow themselves to have access to everything within them, including their fantasies, for fantasies can provide the raw material for their creativity.

Fantasy is the source of all creativity, according to Freud. The true artist, he wrote, "possesses the mysterious power of shaping some particular material until it has become a faithful image of his fantasy," and both artist and audience derive great pleasure from this expression.[6]

Pleasure is but one result of the creatively expressed fantasy. The artist can also inspire and lead his audience in a corresponding journey of wisdom, growth, and self-healing. Freud pointed out that the neurotic person transforms his fantasy into symptoms or neurosis. The creative person takes the path that leads from neurosis to reality through artistic expression. In short, Freud believed creativity was the road away from neurosis toward health.

People fantasize in innumerable ways. Imagine walking briskly down the street on a rainy day and suddenly bursting into dance just like Gene Kelly in *An American in Paris*. Or envision yourself as the tragic Violetta singing her great soliloquy in *La Traviata*; or imagine eloquently exposing corrupt politicians on national television. These fantasies are both harmless and fun, and without a doubt, they make life more interesting.

Fantasy can be much more, however, than mere frivolity. Fantasy is often the creative force behind civilization's inventions, technology, discoveries, and works of art. Fantasy is a major element in children's stories as well as the paintings of artists such as Paul Klee and Marc Chagall and the music of Hector Berlioz, whose *Symphonie Fantastique* was based on his imagined relationship with the actress Harriet Smithson. Novelists such as the Marquis de Sade and Franz Kafka derived "pleasure, consolation and relief" (Freud) from the sadomasochistic fantasies they created to cope with the unbearable reality of their lives. Bob Kane, the creator of the *Batman* comics, indulged himself in fantasies of evil, which were personified through his character of the Joker. Through Kane, the Joker and Batman waged the war of good and evil. The adventure stories of Jules Verne in his *Journey to the Center of the Earth, From the Earth to the Moon,* and *Twenty Thousand Leagues Under the Sea* and the surrealistic tales in H.G. Wells' *Time Machine* depict fantasy in a pleasant vein. The inner experiences people contact through fantasy can run the gamut from painful to pleasurable, but neither pleasure nor pain—nor any other emotion for that matter—should determine the validity of fantasy.

In its highest form, fantasy includes humankind's aspirations toward the ideal—the outgrowth of our deepest wishes. Psychoanalyst Silvano Arieti believed that the search for the ideal represents humanity's highest strivings. It first occurs when the adolescent becomes aware of the enormous discrepancy between the human condition and his ideals. The adolescent, wrote Arieti in *The Magic Synthesis*, "craves for something that he does not have or see: an object that does not exist in his psychological reality. It is by searching for this object that he will continue to grow and give an acceptable meaning to his inner life . . . [This new object will be] an external work that will substitute for the inner fantasy or unrest." His dissatisfaction with the possible and conditional will lead to his conception of "the impossible, the unconditional, the infinitely bigger and the infinitely smaller, the absolute, the whole, nothingness, the real, the unreal, and the increasing expansion of reality. These functions reside in every human being and are particularly pronounced in the creative person."[7]

Fantasies are a forbidden subject for many people because our institutions inhibit us early on from admitting all of our feelings. But cutting yourself off from your fantasy life deprives you of a vast source of inspiration and ideas. It is far more productive and rewarding to allow your fantasies to fully unfold, and then to express them creatively. Was it fantasy that led Marvin Davis, one of the world's richest men, to become the owner of 20th Century Fox? His boyhood, without a doubt, inspired such fantasies. His adventurous, fun-loving parents always took Marvin and his sister Joan to the theater or to the movies, when Broadway was in its heyday. Life was glamorous. And it was always a treat to top off the evening with corned-beef sandwiches at Lindy's, one of New York's most famous delis at that time. Is it mere coincidence that Davis recently opened up the N.Y. Carnegie Deli in Los Angeles? Here was a man who wasn't afraid to turn his fantasies into reality.

Many geniuses have treasured their fantasies. One of them was Einstein, who wrote in a letter to a friend, "When I examine myself and my methods of thought, I come to the conclusion that the gift of fantasy has meant more to me than my talent for absorbing knowledge."[8] If Einstein wasn't afraid of his fantasies, why should you be? By finding an acceptable outlet for them, you can share their treasures, and pleasures, with others. In the process, you may find yourself going beyond the original fantasy into the realm of something new.

As you do the exercises in this chapter, and in the rest of this book, freely draw upon your fantasies and your ability to fantasize.

Exercise 18:
FANTASIZE SOMETHING YOU WANT RIGHT NOW AND MAKE IT COME TRUE CREATIVELY

In this exercise, allow yourself to have your wildest fantasy. Choose a fantasy you wouldn't dare discuss with anyone, and allow yourself to fully indulge in it. Remind yourself, as you write, that no one is looking over your shoulder. When you are finished, you can tear up or burn the papers containing your secret wishes if you wish to. A first-year law student, cowed by an especially sadistic professor, gave himself exactly what he wanted when he wrote the following fantasy. Although he was reluctant to share this fantasy because it betrayed certain wishes that didn't match his ideal view of himself, he did so anyway. He was in a workshop where people encouraged one another to be honest in their creative expression. They had learned that creativity is an acceptable and safe way to express all thoughts and feelings. In addition, he had just listened to Freud's well-known passage describing creativity. Freud regarded creativity as disguised fantasies which the artist works over "in such a way as to make them lose what is too personal about them and repels strangers, and to make it possible for others to share in the enjoyment of them."[9] By letting himself go all the way with his fantasy, the law student found the key to changing an uncomfortable situation.

I am in Professor H's class; he is about to call on me and humiliate me in front of everyone. Suddenly six absolutely gorgeous women, dressed in black leather and high heels and carrying machine guns, burst into the lecture hall and turn their guns on me. They are going to kill me because I have made love to all of them and they are all in love with me. Despite the fact that I might die any second, every man in that room envies me. I talk them out of it by telling them that I love them all. They finally agree that I am so virile and marvelous that it would indeed be a shame for only one woman to have me.

They beg my forgiveness, which I magnanimously grant. Professor H then makes a very slight disparaging remark to me; ordinarily I would take it as a compliment. The women, however, are enraged that anyone would speak to me in such a manner, and turn their machine guns on him. They fire at his feet and he is so afraid that he pees in his pants in front of the whole class. He tries to run away from them but they chase him, firing the whole time; he looks like a frightened rabbit. He trips and falls on his knees and they surround him, guns pointed at his head. He begs them to spare his life, and they finally agree, on the condition that he treats me like the superior being that I am. He agrees, with tears pouring down his cheeks. Each woman kisses me passionately and I tell them I'll meet them after class. I then nonchalantly sit down, as if this sort of thing happens every day.

Writing out his fantasy was a cathartic experience for the student, as well as a highly pleasurable one. And he also got a lesson in consciousness-raising later from the women in the workshop, who accused him of being a male chauvinist pig. After writing out the fantasy, he found that he was no longer so intimidated by the professor, for he had a clear picture in his mind's eye of the teacher frantically scurrying around the classroom in wet trousers. The professor seemed to respond to his change of attitude; while still sarcastic and demanding, he no longer seemed quite so intent on humiliating the student at every opportunity.

A middle-aged woman at first resisted doing the fantasy exercise. She felt she had everything she basically wanted in life and additionally judged it undignified to fantasize at her age. She managed a women's clothing store and had learned to accept responsibility for her own life, now that her husband was dead. However, her real love was repairing antique jewelry. One day, feeling burnt out from other people's demands, and bored besides, she decided to do the fantasy exercise. This was her fantasy:

My son picks me up from work in a limousine. We drive to my house where a chauffeur opens up the car door and the butler opens up my house door. I'm too tired right now to even put the key in the lock. A living room full of stimulating, charming and wonderful people are waiting to greet me with champagne and loving comments. The party is clearly in my honor. I leave the party after an hour, and go upstairs where a lady-in-waiting runs my bath. My guests have magically disappeared. The bathroom is filled with exquisite aromas. After my bath, I dress to kill. My beau comes with orchids and pins them on my dress and he takes me to an extravagantly expensive restaurant, one I would never dream I'd ever go to. The next day I call in sick. I spend the entire day working on my jewelry. Classical music is playing on my new CD.

The upshot of this fantasy was that she went back to work refreshed and energetic. And the next day, without giving it a second thought, she made an important phone call. "I don't know how I had the nerve to do this," she said. "I called up a gentleman who owns a very prestigious antique shop in the area and I talked him into giving me space in his shop for nothing . . . to use as a drop for people to bring in antique jewelry in need of repair. I said I'd stay in the store from one to five on Saturdays to answer all questions about jewelry. I told him it would bring him a lot of business. And he said, 'O.K.' "

Exercise 19:
PLAY WITH YOUR FANTASY

Fantasies are pure expressions of our imaginations, usually created without conscious effort or preconceived ideas. This makes them ideal subjects for creative expression.

Explore your favorite fantasy by expressing it in a medium such as paint, poetry, a story, a play, a novel, a video tape or photograph. If you already work in one of these mediums, try a medium you have not yet explored. Each medium will uncover or highlight disparate aspects of the fantasy which can add great richness and depth when translated into your chosen method of expression. This is also an excellent way to unblock yourself when you're stuck in your own medium, since it forces you to approach the new situation without your usual self-expectations. It's more acceptable to fail on unfamiliar territory.

Imagine yourself identifying fully with each character and part of your fantasy. The oneness with each element will give you the fullest experience of it. Allow your fantasy to grow and change as you play with it. If something new comes up, don't analyze it or try to decide whether or not you should proceed in that direction; just follow it wherever it goes. Not only can your fantasy evolve and change, but also your ideas and preconceptions about expressing it. Let your view of your method of expression become as big as possible. See if the ideas that arise from using one medium can be translated to another. Keep yourself as open as possible; if you feel you want to go in an entirely new direction when you switch mediums, go with that. The important thing is to be spontaneous and experimental.

If you have difficulty coming up with a fantasy you want to work with, recall one from your childhood. A history teacher chose to explore her childhood fantasy of playing in the clouds.

I fly to the land of the clouds, far up in the sky. The clouds are shimmering colors of late sunset, dark pink shot with rivers of gold, with the texture of fine silk thread spun like cotton candy. Walking on them in bare feet is a sensual delight. Above, the sky is the backdrop for billions of stars arrayed in celestial pictures. Their brilliance reflects a white glow on everything around me.

Everything ever created, and more, is available here, but none of it is visible except when desired. Restrictions of time and space are shrugged off like damp overcoats. There is beauty, always and everywhere. The people are dressed in graceful white gowns, ancient, mythic clothing. They speak in lyrical cadences that would sound artificial if they weren't so perfectly natural. Everyone exudes a gentle warmth; they know they are all equally exceptional and assume the same for everyone they meet. There is no fear or envy, just a light, pervading air of contentment. Everything is easy, the way it should be. It occurs to me that this could be heaven.

I approach a middle-aged man and question him about that. He chuckles. "Does it matter? Are you happy? Better yet, is there any other place you'd rather be?"

"Yes, yes, no." But I still want an answer to my question. There are centuries of theology, philosophy, and culture (not to mention the now-questionable status of my mortality) at stake here; a conversation is in order.

He tells me that heaven and hell are the same place; the only distinction is whether you're happy there or not. For someone who gets a thrill from subjugating others, it's hell to be forced to live inside your god self in a place where everyone is equally powerful.

Intrigued by what emerged from writing this fantasy, the teacher decided to explore it in other mediums. She borrowed her eight-year-old's set of watercolors and painted the land of the clouds:

I started with pink, yellow, and orange, and soon found myself adding different hues of blue, green, and purple as well, a kaleidoscope of colors. I wasn't used to working with paints, and so my initial brush strokes were merely straight lines. As I permitted myself to spontaneously play, I began to make circular spirals and overlap the colors. I began to feel very excited; I had the definite sensation that I was expressing something, but I couldn't verbalize what it was. It was my first direct experience with the world of ideas that can't be put into words, and I felt like an explorer in a new territory . . . I then decided to turn my fantasy into a dance. Pushing past my initial feelings of foolishness, I began moving as if I were walking on clouds. As I let myself go, my movements became increasingly expansive, I could *feel* the sensation of infinity, and that the experience opened up a new spiritual dimension to the land of the clouds. I then "danced" the feeling of being forced to live inside a moral, loving god self when you don't want to, and felt waves of emotion wash over me: frustration, claustrophobia, anger, fear, bitterness. These feelings led to resignation, acceptance of fate, and a curiosity about the god self. I then danced an exploration of my god self, which became a ritualistic, joyous, spiritual rebirth.

At the end of the exercise, she was exhausted but elated. Expressing her fantasy in these different media had revealed modes of perception she had never known existed. She saw that there were aspects of things that couldn't be discovered through reading alone but, once discovered through other media, could be expressed in words. Now she often imagines herself dancing or drawing her new subject matter, and she invariably finds that it reveals new dimensions of her subject that can then be communicated to her students.

Exploring your fantasy world can provide multiple answers and solutions to problems. One way to realize your potential and enhance your creative growth is to continue generating ideas even after you think you've found the "perfect" one. Approach situations and problems from a variety of angles, not just the most obvious or seemingly appropriate one. Give yourself permission to be illogical, ridiculous, wrong. An idea that is impossible to implement can always be reworked or altered later on, and it may inspire other, more workable ideas and directions. Remember, the most original idea may not be the first one.

Free association is one way to generate multiple solutions. The following two exercises can help you adjust to this kind of thinking. And remember, the great Leonardo da Vinci himself studied clouds to find new ideas for his paintings. In the first exercise (Exercise A), choose an object from nature—a cloud, a tree, a rock—and look at it. What shapes and images do you see? Write down each picture as it occurs to you, then clear your mind and allow another picture to appear. See how many different images can emerge from the same object.

A man gazed at a tree outside his window and came up with the following images contained in the configuration of the branches:

An elephant

A baseball pitcher

A vase

A man hanging from a noose

A lady's head

The letter "E"

A Scottish terrier's face

A teddy bear

Sylvester the cat

A bow tie

A high-heeled boot

An outstretched hand

He reported that after the first two images he felt stuck and almost gave up, but he decided to make himself look at the tree for five minutes before calling it quits. He said that he was blank for the first two or three minutes but then felt something open up in him, and all of a sudden he was flooded with a stream of images. He felt he could have gone on forever listing the pictures that he saw without exhausting the possibilities, and he experienced the exercise as a concrete and eye-opening example of how vast the array of creative options could be.

A painter did a variation on this exercise. She too selected clouds as her subject and then listed the following associations to them:

Clouds

A cloud of dust and a hearty Hi Ho Silver
Silver Cloud Rolls Royce
Clouds in the sky over a Third Avenue
   parking lot, looking downtown
Little fish-scale clouds in a mackerel
   sky from summer camp
Clouds moving fast across the night sky,
   a coming storm
Healthy, happy summer, late clouds in
   Maine, with children calling game
   words to each other on the hill
Clouds outlined in graphite on a landscape
   of Michigan
Horizontal grey clouds in a pink yellow,

green sky . . .
Sunset at Montauk.

She then made a collage from these various images. And it proved to be vastly different from her usual work.

A woman did this variation of the exercise with a piece of driftwood:

Driftwood
A small brown baby animal head asleep at the end of a winding wooden pole. It's the deep sleep of innocence. The other side is a demon with a grimacing smile. It has large lower jaws, small ears, and a grey, snake-like body with a gentle twist. It's laughing to itself; it has a secret. As I look longer, it looks more benign.

From the top it looks like a flatworm. It's about six inches long, with very beautiful sinuous movements within the wood. The baby animal side is hugging itself; it has a rudimentary tail piece. The monster demon side, now more benign, is the baby's mother. So baby and mother are incorporated into the same person, after birth. How can the two become individuated if one body contains the two? It's like mother and baby are Siamese twins, but one side of the face is the daughter and the other side is the mother.

Looking straight on, the divisions aren't so clear. On the left, there's a hand and arm under the chin, the eye on the right is crying, and there's a huge ear or growth on top of the head, but it's not grotesque. There's a snout. The face is noncommittal and certainly not menacing. Perhaps it's the adult both these elements grew up into. Actually it has a sweet look.

When I close my eyes, the image monster
comes towards me, and stops short, wanting to
converse. "Do you like me?" it asks. "I don't
know yet," I reply. "How can you be so mean,
so unfeeling?" it asks me. Me: "I can't tell what
you consist of yet. Are you a baby, a mother, or
a monster? You're a mystery."

Suddenly she sits down; she's now wearing a
small ruffled skirt, and smiles and starts playing
with mudpies. "Will you join me?" she asks. My
first response is, "No, you stupid monster."
Maybe she would make a mudpie out of me.
Then out of each mudpie grows beautiful flowers
of every color. She then turns into a goddess and
weeps at a new moon appearing thinly in the
darkened sky. She becomes a large windshield
wiper swinging from one side of the sky to the
other.

This exercise proved to be quite revelatory for this woman;
not only did it challenge her imagination but she saw that
her fear of what she perceived as ugly was blocking her
personal growth. She learned that when she disowned her
uncomfortable feelings, she remained stuck, whereas
when she took the risk of accepting these feelings (e.g.,
seeing the monster as stupid and then saying "no" to it),
she could move into new unexpected experiences. As a
result of the exercise, she felt freer and did not censor
content that she had previously avoided. She also decided
to take more chances in her personal and social life and
would say how she truly felt rather than give the polite
response she had been accustomed to. She discovered that
her relationships became more rewarding and she continued to feel more authentic.

Assumptions and habits are necessary in our lives so that

we don't have to relearn everything every day, but they stifle creativity. The importance of fantasy is that it opens up parts of ourselves we are not in the habit of using. The next exercise (Exercise B) can help you to perceive things freshly again as well as stimulate you to create multiple solutions to problems. Select an ordinary household object: a glass, an ashtray, a hanger, anything. Now pretend that you've never seen it before and have no idea what it is or what it does. Pick it up and examine it thoroughly, put it in different positions. Then make a list of all the possible uses for it other than the customary one, no matter how absurd. In essence, this exercise transports you back to your childhood, when you were seeing things for the first time and didn't know the function of every object you saw.

Two newlyweds were in a quandary. They had just moved into a charming new apartment that had an outdoor patio, protected by a gate. They soon learned to their horror that drug dealers and other undesirables would jump over the gate and do illicit deals right next to their window late at night. The police were never around when it happened. John, the husband, contacted the city's Landmarks Preservation Commission to get permission to build a fence, but he learned it would be costly and take at least six months before the plan could be approved. Oddly enough, it was through doing this exercise that a solution occurred to him. He chose a clear drinking glass as his object and listed the following possible uses:

A perch for birds

A candle mold

A device to add height to other objects

A device to protect your eyes

A weapon

A planter

A home for insects

An exercise toy for hamsters

A rolling pin

A glove

A baking pan for bread, pastry, etc.

A shovel

A butterfly net

A lampshade

A protective covering for plants

The last phrase, "a protective covering for plants," stayed in John's mind, and when he looked at the gate again, he envisioned a wall of greenery. He learned that a thorny bush known as fire thorn could be used to keep out intruders; since this vegetation was not a stationary structure, it was not necessary for him to get permission from the Landmarks Preservation Commission to install it. The bush's attractiveness did not belie its lethal function—to inflict injury on anyone who attempted to go beyond the boundary it designated and trespass on private property. The solution worked and the couple were able to enjoy their new home in privacy and safety. Not only can an exercise of this nature stretch the imagination, it also points out how solutions to problems come to us when we are in the creative mode.

Make fantasy a daily part of your life. It can immediately bring you in touch with what you want, and what you need. And it can be a consistently rewarding source of pleasure and creativity.

PART THREE

Illumination

8

THREE SURE-FIRE TECHNIQUES FOR "HOT" FLASHES

When you want to penetrate deeply and quickly into your unconscious, these three techniques will produce immediate insights—"hot" flashes—from your dreams. Since every dream is a visual expression, it helps to think of your dream as a photograph, or even a movie. The plot, imagery, and symbols all provide information about your immediate and often deepest concern. A dream can be like the riddle of the Sphinx; once you uncover its secret, you become free from various conflicts in your life and your happiness is measurably increased. The first exercise is great fun to do and brings you directly in touch with your creativity.

Exercise 20:
THE NONSENSE RHYME

You can do this exercise at any time, with any dream or with any problem. It's especially effective when you're at a creative impasse, when everything else has failed and your mind is a blank. Setting up a nonsense structure of expression removes all expectations for any kind of relevant meaning. Anything, no matter how ridiculous, can pop up. This rhyming exercise, with its totally arbitrary structure, removes your responsibility for what arises. It bypasses any fear that something unknown or ominous from your unconscious will suddenly loom up and confront you. Thus, wild ideas are able to surface without being criticized or stifled. And your creative choices are infinite.

First, think of a particularly interesting symbol or image from a dream, and write it down. Keep the description relatively short and allow yourself to feel the rhythm. Then write down another image or idea that rhymes with the first, and keep on going. Move quickly and don't think about making sense; this is not an exercise in poetry. Whenever you get stuck, free associate or respond to the previous phrase and begin rhyming again. Don't try to lead yourself in any direction or invent anything clever or meaningful; the topic and ideas will emerge of their own accord. Your only thought should be to create a rhyme.

A woman had a dream in which she was weaving dollar bills out of green thread. She wrote this nonsense rhyme based upon that image:

Make a buck. Good luck. Poor life sucks.
But from duties you still can't duck.

Any good luck can turn into muck.
Is there good luck in the muck?
Yes, there is, if there are bucks.
Is luck all bucks?
Or is there more once that's been shucked?
Soft of heart but mind like puck.
  I won't fall for that humble junk.
You can't tell how big my hunk.
I'll fight for the biggest chunk.
Come too close and your head I'll dunk.
But I'm lonely in my lavish bunk.
Shall I share it with some lucky punk?
No, the last one's armpits really stunk.
And one might try to steal a chunk.
If I want to protect my hunk,
must I live like a pure monk,
and never share my double bunk,
and always watch for beer-bellied lunks?
Having good luck can put you in a funk.

This woman, who had once studied to be a concert violinist, was working at a high-paying research job. She had little or no time to play the violin and made excuses that her job took up all her time. She often complained about how unhappy she was. The startling bit of information that emerged from writing this nonsense rhyme was that she felt greedy about everything: money, possessions, fame, love—but especially ownership. This kept her not only from the violin but from companionship. She was astounded at this insight. After she wrote the nonsense rhyme, she began to consider her options. Was she to have comfort and loneliness at the expense of creative fulfillment and companionship? She decided she wanted the latter more than money. But could she support herself on less? Yes, she decided, if she adjusted her lifestyle by giving up some of her activities such as theater subscriptions and frequent dinner parties. After a few weeks of reflecting on this decision, she approached her boss and asked if he'd be willing to let her work only three days rather than a full week. Business was not good, and he was relieved to cut down on his expenses. She now would have a chunk of uninterrupted time to play the violin. And she soon began doing the thing she loved most.

A lawyer who yearned to write a novel was terribly frustrated; he couldn't even get the first word down on paper. He made many attempts but always gave up in despair. Finally, he forced himself to sit in front of a blank sheet of paper, for an entire day if necessary, to write just one page of his novel. This was a step in the right direction, and he did it. But he criticized his writing as tight and self-conscious. That night he dreamt that he was eating a huge ice cream cone. The cone kept refilling itself with new, unusual, and delicious flavors. He wrote the following nonsense rhyme, triggered by the ice cream cone:

I wonder if this joy will last.
I'm not too sure, it came so fast.
It's not the same as in the past.
It's deeper, like a great repast.
    It feels like sureness.
It's not an oven or a furnace.
    More like air,
An answer to a prayer.
Like a fount, from an old soothsayer.
The facts are within. Not over there.
I'll get them out with work and care.
    I'll let it flow, all *yes*, no *no*.
Words like fireflies. All aglow.
Not too fast. Not too slow.
Like gentle breezes blow.

The problem is to make some dough.
Without the need to sell my soul.
The child will out. And roll, roll, roll.
   Down hills and valleys.
Through streets and alleys.
No accounts or tallies.
Just larks and sallies.
   Into free territory. To write a story.
Not for fame. Not for glory.
Just for fun. For art and more [pronounced to
   rhyme with *glory*].
   For my good feeling. To send me reeling.
Up to the ceiling. One that's not peeling, I hope.
   But not for wealth. More for my health.
Not got by stealth. But because I dealt . . .
   myself the true hand.
To make my life grand. And do away with bland . . .
   ness and banality.
   If life is work, it must be worth
   the dearth of ease.
   To please myself, and tease
   the fates who call us.
Ingrates who walk on the edge of the ledge.

Although he was not aware of it at the time, the very act of writing melted some of his resistance. And when he wrote the nonsense rhyme, he was delighted with how easily it came to him and became convinced that he had a true flair with words. By allowing his humor to come through, his writing became alive and natural. He didn't sound academic and stilted as he did when he wrote his law briefs. He was so inspired by this rhyming exercise that he began using all his free time to write the first chapter of his novel. It took him a week. And he was eager to continue writing.

Exercise 21:
IMPULSE DRAWING

Working from your impulses, such as doodling, stream-of-consciousness writing, etc., enables you to generate ideas without overthinking them. Allow yourself to choose a given dream, return to the feeling state or situation of your dream, and then start drawing. Let your impulses take over. The key is to work without stopping, not even for a second. That way you can't censor yourself and evaluate what you're doing. Give yourself total freedom to do anything, forget about expectations, goals, and judgments. Create from the immediacy of the moment, experience the freedom of moving instantly from idea to action.

During this exercise, deep feelings may be stirred. Allow all your thoughts and emotions, no matter how angry or sad, to surface. Don't cut yourself off from them. Work through them by continuing to draw until the emotion resolves itself. By allowing yourself the full experience of your feeling you'll be able to transform it into a source of creative inspiration and energy.

A woman who was becoming more and more displeased with her lover dreamt that she was standing at the top of a hill. Dogs began climbing up the hill and looking at her menacingly. She kept on walking down the hill, and much to her surprise, the dogs made a path for her. Then they went away. The meaning of this dream was unclear until she got back into the feeling of the dream by doing an impulse drawing of it (Figure 4). As the picture emerged, she realized that she was afraid of the dogs attacking and biting her. Her lover was a very critical "biting" person. And when she realized that she had to

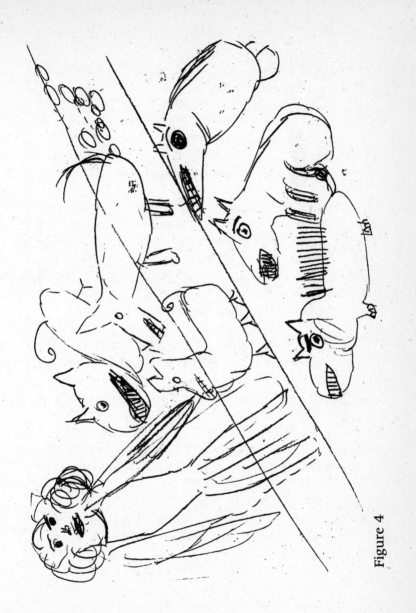

Figure 4

be careful of her every move for fear she would be attacked for it, she decided this was not the man for her. She wasted little time in ending the relationship and felt great relief and freedom to move on.

By doing this exercise, an account executive learned why a current misunderstanding with a coworker was evoking such tumultuous fear and rage in him. In his dream, he is sharing some of his ideas with his boss; an acquaintance (whom he later realized represented his coworker) is contradicting him in front of his boss. The dream disturbed him so much that when he woke up, he decided to express his feelings about it. He picked up his five-year-old child's crayon and colored an abstract, jagged shape over and over, trying to make as solid a block of color as he could. He worked with such intensity that the crayon was just a tiny stub when he finished. Discussing it later in his creativity group, he said:

> While I was doing it I suddenly remembered a time when I was very young and in school. Our class project was coloring in a big map of the whole world, and everyone was assigned certain sections. I was coloring in a red section, and I remembered that I worked very hard to stay within the lines and do a good job. Afterwards I was very proud of what I had done; it was perfectly and neatly colored.
>
> But when it came time for the teacher to hand out the next assignments on the map, she wouldn't give me another section because she thought that I had also colored in a red section that was very messy. I tried to explain to her that I hadn't done the messy part, I had only done the neat one. But she wouldn't listen to me and wouldn't let me do any more. I was so angry

and hurt and, worst of all, frustrated and helpless. I tried everything I knew, but it was impossible for me to convince her of the truth. Not
only didn't I get recognized for the good work
that I was so proud of, but I also got punished
for something I didn't do—that was the opposite
of what I had done.

He then realized that it wasn't so much the actual misunderstanding that was currently bothering him, but
rather a deep fear that he would once again be helpless
and deficient in getting the truth out into the open, and
would again be wrongly punished. Realizing the cause of
his anger and concern, he was able to calm himself by
reminding himself that he was no longer a powerless child
and was fully capable of handling the situation. Unfortunately, traumatizing childhood experiences have a tendency to linger on in the unconscious and continue to
blight our lives, if there is nobody to talk them over with
at the time they occur.

This exercise provides a marvelous opportunity to view
the contents of your unconscious before they're censored,
edited, or mentally rewritten.

Exercise 22:
WORK FROM A NEGATIVE FEELING AND EXPRESS IT FULLY

One of the mixed blessings of being human is the wide
range of emotions we're capable of feeling. While some
of these emotions are delightful, such as love, joy, and
elation, there also are emotions that some people consider

to be dark or negative. Anger, fear, anxiety, shame, jealousy, hurt, guilt are just some of the feelings that fall into this category. The creative person who delves deeply into his or her inner life and its turmoil often seems to experience more of these feelings than others do.

Unfortunately, our early training, our families, and society have taught us that many of these feelings are wrong . . , largely out of their own fear of feelings or their need to control us by suppressing ours. However, these feelings are *not* bad; in fact, they serve important purposes. Anxiety, for example, warns us that we feel danger, even though the danger may be something from our past that we no longer remember and that can no longer hurt us. Guilt helps us to be better human beings by keeping us in touch with the feelings of others. It's only when our defenses become bigger than the purposes for which they are intended that problems arise.

The feelings themselves are not "bad"; what *is* bad is acting on these feelings in inappropriate ways, indulging in behavior that is destructive to ourselves and others. And while acting out some feelings is not to our advantage, not seeing where they come from prevents us from truly dealing with them. We need to learn how to express these feelings constructively. Otherwise they build up until we explode, or turn them against ourselves in the form of illnesses or emotional disorders that prevent us from growing and leading fulfilled lives.

Emotions are not static. There's a natural tendency for us to express them. When we don't, we become blocked in many areas of our lives, including the creative ones. When we suppress so-called "unacceptable" feelings, they manifest themselves instead in physical ailments, discomfort, and stress. In Exercise 22, you will be able to release this repressive force by giving vent to your feelings. Creativity is a completely safe way to do this. Compare the energy you use to suppress a feeling to a dam holding in water. If there is too much water (energy), the dam will overflow and lead to destruction. If instead of suppressing the feeling you purposefully release it—like a dam releases a pent up flow—then the energy is available for creative purposes.

In the closing phase of his psychoanalytic treatment, a patient of the prominent Swiss psychoanalyst Alice Miller told her how important it was for him to experience his negative feelings: "It was not the beautiful or pleasant feelings which gave me new insight but the ones against which I had fought most strongly: feelings which made me experience myself as shabby, petty, mean, helpless, humiliated, demanding, resentful or confused. And above all sad and lonely. However, it was precisely from these experiences, which I had avoided for so long, that I gained the certainty of understanding, stemming from the core of my being, something which I could not have learnt from any book!"[10]

Experiencing *all* our feelings enables us to live meaningfully, completely, and creatively. Would Shakespeare have been such a superlative writer, such a genius, if he had not intimately known the feelings he expressed through his characters: the obsessions, rage, revenge, envy, desire for power, ruthlessness, fear, and cowardice? It was Shakespeare's deep, unflinching exploration of these facets of human nature that gave his work the universal appeal and meaning that makes it still powerful and relevant today. And he had to experience, confront, and accept these feelings in himself in order to incorporate them so deftly in his characters.

Filmmaker Ingmar Bergman is another example of an artist who has used his "negative" feelings to enrich his work. As Ira Progoff, creator of the Intensive Journal process, explains, Bergman let "the demons come out so that they could speak and act. That was the only way that he would be able to establish a relationship with them. Only in that way, too, when they had expressed their need, then only could their negative power be neutralized."[11]

Some people take their negative feelings and sing them out in the shower. A woman who does this says it bolsters her self-esteem and keeps her from denying her problems and pretending to be happy. Negative feelings can be the raw material for our creativity regardless of what direction our creativity may take. Instead of rejecting these feelings we can embrace them and use them as our inspiration and source of creative energy. Exercise 22 gives us a structure with which to explore our demons and dark feelings as well as release our creativity. The idea for the exercise was inspired by anthropologist Kilton Stewart's accounts of the Senoi, a tribe of Malaysian aborigines. Stewart described them as a remarkable people who from childhood learned to fully experience their intense feelings in their dreams—their fears as well as their pleasures. During a dream they expressed their feelings fully. For example, they might confront a savage tiger and, despite their terror, fight that tiger to the death. Or they might encounter an erotic object and copulate and reach orgasm. Then they ask both dream enemies and lovers for gifts. The gift would be something that they truly wanted. Thus, they exercised creativity during their dreams and later, the next day, they actualized these dreams in their waking hours. They would dance their dream dances, tell their dream poems or stories, implement their dream inventions, make their dream costumes, practice their new dream skills, and try out their dream solutions to problems.

This was a brilliant solution to the age-old problem of how to handle feelings. And whether or not this was a description of an actual Senoi practice or a fabrication on

Stewart's part, it does not in any way deter from its effectiveness as a method for transforming feeling into creativity and well-being. (Current researchers are questioning whether Stewart attributed to the Senoi an invented framework in which to express his own dream psychology and mastery—much as the Don Juan tales of Carlos Castaneda—or whether such a civilization, embodying these ideas, did indeed exist.)

In structuring Exercise 22, I have done a variation on these techniques. When you awaken, begin writing from the feeling in your dream; express it fully until it runs its course. Feelings are not always apparent in dreams. We may awaken only with the memory of a bizarre story or image, in which case, the feelings are contained within the imagery itself, and it takes dreamwork to unlock them. But in some dreams the feelings are obvious—in the nightmare, for example, or the erotic dream. Anxiety is another emotion commonly experienced in dreams and benefits well from this exercise, because you can discover what is causing the anxiety. Other dreams touch off feelings such as grief, horror, disgust, hurt, helplessness, rage, and hopelessness.

The feelings that come out of dreams are crucial because dreams are direct messages from the unconscious—and therefore are the source of our creativity.

Fred was experiencing grief in almost every major area of his life. Not only had his fiancée broken off their engagement, but also he had not been offered the promotion he deserved. He had worked for eight years as a paralegal assistant for the same company. His immediate superior had left the company and the job needed to be filled. Fred felt he deserved the position because of his years of hard work, loyalty, and long hours. He was stunned to learn that his boss had given the job to a recent employee who had managed to make friends with everyone. Fred knew he had difficulty selling himself, and he tended to be diffident about asking for anything he wanted.

The night his fiancée left him, he dreamt he was back in his childhood home in Connecticut. In his dream his parents were present and so were their best friends, very successful people whom his parents put on a pedestal. A peacock without feathers stood on the porch looking sad and about to die. It was ugly without its feathers. And nobody paid any attention to it.

Fred awoke from this dream feeling depressed, realizing that *he* was the plucked peacock in the dream. He decided to do the exercise, expressing all of his feelings from the the point of view of the peacock.

> Here I am naked, featherless, and ashamed. I want everyone's love and admiration, but no one will look at me. I'm a nonentity, a nothing. How did I get to be this way? Look over there, my parents standing there ignoring me as if I don't exist. Or perhaps they're ashamed of me too. I can tell by the way Mom is eyeing me with that critical expression. I can't seem to ever be able to please her, though I try. What do I have to do, become Albert Schweitzer? Get my name in the newspapers? Lose my life heroically? Maybe if I did something wonderful, I could change the expressions on their faces. Maybe I could suddenly die in a car accident. Then they might be sorry that they treated me with such disdain, and beg my forgiveness, after it was too late.
>
> I certainly have to go to extremes to win their love. It makes me wonder what's wrong with them! What makes them so perfect! How could loving parents have made me feel so worthless?

According to the dream I was born a peacock, a beautiful one, until they stripped me of what I rightfully deserve—my pride and self-worth.

As Fred wrote this, he first began to feel sad, then deeply angry at the unfairness and cruelty of people who were supposed to care about him but were too involved in themselves to even notice him. As his rage mounted and he justifiably felt all the associated feelings of mourning for what he was entitled to as a child but never got, he envisioned the peacock's feathers lying next to him in a pile. With rage, he realized only *he* could save himself. He imagined thrusting each feather into himself, where it belonged. He cried out in elation each time he thrust in his imaginary feather. He ended up feeling so high that he believed now he could do anything he wanted. One of his wishes was to see his boss the next day and tell him he was quitting. He no longer cared that he might be kicked out of a secure, familiar place. The anger that triggered off his depression was freed and mobilized him to action.

The next day he strutted into his boss's office like the proud peacock he really was and gave the boss his news in a calm and collected manner. His boss was shocked at Fred's announcement and at the change in his demeanor. He had always liked Fred but had thought he could push him around indefinitely. When Fred announced he was quitting, the boss replied, "Wait a minute. You're a valuable employee here. I don't want to lose you. Let me think this over." Fred nonchalantly said "Okay." The next day, the boss offered him a higher position and a hefty raise in salary. Fred accepted. Even more important, he felt good about himself. His new attitude became apparent. And people began to notice him for the first time.

An artist who had just broken up with her boyfriend

dreamt they were together again. This only served to reinforce all the pain she was feeling: the abandonment, the anger, the betrayal by someone she had thought was her friend, and the self-reproachments for putting herself in a situation where she could be hurt. She tried to deal with the pain by understanding it, but that didn't work. So she made a drawing (Figure 5).

Afterward, she explained: "I let the characters speak for me outrageously. Putting it down on the page externalized it for me. It helped me see my part in it. The little girl in me said, 'Why didn't you protect me?' I was angry at *me* for not protecting that little girl. By expressing my worst fears and feelings about myself, they didn't have to keep flying around in my head. I nailed them down."

Another variation on this exercise is to express the feeling in the dream and demand a gift, as the Senoi did. A woman dreamt that she was snubbed and rejected by her social peers at a party. Writing from this feeling of rejection, she realized that she wanted to be so outstanding that she could ignore other people and get away with it. She associated being special with being able to be obnoxious and yet still not be snubbed by others. This awareness taught her that she had much more control over being rejected than she had thought.

Then she asked the people in her dream for a gift; they gave her a blue ribbon. This stood as the symbol of being first. She made a painting out of the vivid blue she saw in the ribbon, which she described in the following way:

> The blue is a painting starting with the lines in all the different blues, and then taking off and creating the beauty of all the blues, like cobalt, and navy, and robin's egg blues. Then I accented the blues by adding blacks, whites, and orange. Dissonance, composition, bringing out the beauty

Figure 5

of all the blues. I want to shock everyone with
the very power of the blues. I want to push the
love of blue to the front.

She described how she usually handled her feelings: "Ordinarily when I go to parties, I feel like a bad, inferior,
rejected trouble-maker—selfish and insecure, deservedly
rejected by others for making fun of them. But now I
changed it completely with this exercise by getting the gift
of the blue ribbon, and by doing the blue painting. It's
amazing."

A woman doctor dreamt that as she was addressing her
colleagues at a medical convention, the audience began
to fade away. She was unable to see them but knew they
were there. Knowing that *they* could see *her* made her feel
vulnerable and unprotected. When she awakened, she
grabbed her pencil and pad and explored in writing her
fear of public accountability in the following passage:

I feel that everything I know and do is of such
superficial depth, like a thin and fragile facade
which would fold away to reveal a limp, fleshy
mass that is unable to protect itself or resist abuse
and contempt. This mass is without limbs or skin.
Where is the commitment and drive which will
give structure and form to the mush that is me?
Can I choose one or two goals and simply pursue
them mindlessly?

When she asked for a gift, the image that came to her was
"a nude ravioli, filled with ricotta cheese and spinach,
sprinkled with a little nutmeg, and looking very vulnerable on a big plate." She thought it was an odd gift, but
went ahead and expressed it creatively by writing a little
story about it from its point of view. This was the result:

I could tell she was disappointed. She wanted a pasta dish as an appetizer and the waiter suggested spaghetti with tomato sauce or *me*, the ravioli. She selected me out of curiosity. I think she thought there would be pasta in the dish, but there I was—a delicate mass of ricotta and spinach with more than a hint of nutmeg. I was resting comfortably in my butter sauce, quite shamelessly really, a pale oblong entity trying to pass myself off as whole and true even though I didn't have a pasta skin. I think she had her doubts but she started to eat. The house wine was good and flattered my delicate nature. I could tell she enjoyed me, even with the reservation of thinking there was too much nutmeg.

My real glory occurred with another woman. She had developed an acquired taste for nude ravioli and ordered me as a main dish. I once heard her say she was fond of nutmeg. She once told a companion that I reminded her of a drawing course she once took. The technique consisted of slow shading, which began at any point in the subject and expanded out. No lines or sketches were allowed, nor could the pencil be lifted; the whole was in the part. She said she originally found it difficult to conceive a drawing as a radiation out from one point. It required a relaxed focus, and no worrying about proportions, relationships, or structures. She told her friend that I, the nude ravioli, inspired her to go back to basics and stop worrying about where she might wind up professionally and in specific areas. "Ah yes," said her companion as he took a sample of me, "the importance of the path and not the goal."

The doctor enjoyed this exercise immensely. She also learned that seeing herself as nude ravioli reflected her awareness of being exposed in front of others and hoping to please them all as a delectable dish. Her conflicting wishes—on the one hand, to please others, and on the other hand, to achieve recognition in her field—kept her stuck. The first wish, she thought, required self-annihilation to give others what they wanted; the second, she believed, demanded an assertive personality. No wonder she was terrified of public speaking. She always worried about which personality would dominate. Neither one, in her opinion, was acceptable. By doing this exercise, she was able to view herself as a special person: delicate but subtle (yet, for that reason, often mistaken as "mush"). And as she continued writing the exercise, she created situations in which others also recognized her value. This ultimately gave her the confidence to be herself when she spoke publicly. The new confidence enabled her to speak more eloquently and convincingly than ever before. She began to look forward to her speaking engagements and spiced up her talks with humor. She also continued to write amusing short stories.

Expressing the feelings of our dreams through writing or drawing can lead to creative works in and of themselves. Almost without exception, this expression can lead to new perceptions of oneself, resolutions of conflicts, and new creative directions in one's life.

9

TURN A NEGATIVE REALITY INTO A DREAM

Nothing challenges one's creativity more than a nagging, persistent problem. The problem can be as prosaic as deciding whether to invite your mother-in-law to dinner or as monumental as recovering from the loss of a loved one. Problems may pop up in any area of life, and in the more traditionally creative ones too. It takes creativity on the part of a hostess to turn an argument between guests into playful persiflage, for a writer to concoct the unexpected ending to a suspense thriller. Creative problem-solving enables a single working mother to make time for a rewarding social life, for a painter to work out problems of composition. Whatever your problem, it can be your passport to creativity because it involves the most central concerns of your life.

Problems have a habit of lingering on until they're

solved. They can haunt your waking and dreaming hours. If only you could be like the proverbial oyster who secretes a magnificent pearl around an irritating grain of sand, creating beauty out of adversity! Well, you could! One of the immediate results of doing these exercises is the gaining of control over a problem that seems to be *out* of control.

The first step is to relinquish the solutions you've repeatedly tried that never work. Try something new instead, such as thinking about your problem as if it were a dream. By doing so, you can explore previously unknown or inaccessible aspects of life's difficulties, thus opening up new methods of quieting them. Dreams can magically lead you right to the trouble spots and signal answers that never occurred to you while you were awake.

Exercise 23:
WRITE YOUR PROBLEM AS A DREAM

Write out your problem as if it were a dream and then do a dream exercise with it. You don't have to work with an actual dream. As you invent the dream to match the actual situation, your imagination will conjure up different modes of thinking and feeling. The exercise will take you off-guard and enable you to view your problem from a new perspective. There are any number of dreamwork techniques you can use, and all are effective with waking life troubles. For now, try the techniques used in the examples below or refer to those in the previous chapter, "Three Sure-fire Techniques for 'Hot' Flashes."

A woman who was having a difficult time with her new boss was losing her battle to keep her job. She was a recent divorcée with creative aspirations. She wrote this description of her problem, then did a dream exercise with it:

Problems with My Boss

My alimony has run out and for the first time in my life I'm supporting myself; I haven't worked full-time in eight years. I recently got a job as the executive secretary to a high-level advertising executive in a large ad agency. Like so many self-proclaimed "creative" people, he is self-indulgent and irresponsible. He rarely comes into the office, is invariably late for his appointments, changes his mind constantly about everything, and makes even the tiniest chores impossible by not giving me enough, or even correct, information. I'm continually calling people to apologize and make excuses for him, taking heat from everyone mad at him, and fielding questions from his colleagues who want to know where he is and why he isn't where he's supposed to be. It's no secret that he's unhappy in his job and will be leaving soon to form his own agency.

I've been here for two months and I think I've done a pretty good job, all things considered. I admit I've made a few mistakes, but nothing drastic. He's never complimented me or given me any validation for anything I've done. As a matter of fact, he's never really talked to me.

Yesterday his assistant told me that he wanted me out in two weeks. Not only didn't he have the nerve to tell me this in person, he didn't even come into the office. I was stunned and extremely hurt. During my second week on the job his assistant told me that he wanted to fire me, but nothing happened and I was certain that things had improved. I have no idea what I am doing wrong. I called him at home and tried to discuss it with him, telling him I really needed the job, but he was aloof and evasive. I found out today that he's angry at me for confronting him about it.

I'm very upset; this is so unfair. I don't like working for him but I do like this company; the money is good, I've made friends, and I need the security. I know he wanted an older, experienced secretary with no aspirations of doing anything but running after him and wiping his nose. But I wanted the chance to show him that I could do that and more. If I'm fired now I won't complete my three-month probation period at the company. That means I'll have a harder time getting another job there. I don't know why he can't keep me until he leaves the company; then I could fulfill the probation requirements. I think what he's doing is mean and cowardly.

She then chose the dreamwork technique of rewriting the dream from the other character's point of view. This method can put you inside the character and enable you to see yourself and the dream situation from someone else's perspective. In addition, the other characters in a dream often represent parts of yourself you don't wish to look at. This method can allow the hidden critical and self-attacking parts of yourself to come out of hiding while they express themselves fully and you listen without a need to be defensive.

Boss's Point of View

That's exactly what I didn't want. I knew I'd regret letting myself be pressured into hiring her. It's not that she's bad, she just isn't an experienced executive secretary. She views herself as a "creative" person and sees this job as a stepping-stone to something else, probably my job. Being my secretary should be her only goal. I don't want to feel funny about asking her to do boring or personal chores; I know she resents it and wants to be doing more important things.

I need someone who already knows the advertising business and corporate structure, and can take care of me with a minimum of instruction and care. Yes, she did a lot of things right, but so what? None of it was particularly difficult, or at least it wouldn't have been if she was experienced. I don't think I should be expected to make a big fuss congratulating her when she does something correctly; that's her job. And she does make mistakes, and needs instruction in how large companies function. I'm not blaming her for this, she's bright and tries hard, but I see no reason why I can't have the kind of secretary I want.

These are crazy, uncertain times for me, and I need a secretary who's like the Rock of Gilbraltar. I'm too busy to want to know her as a person; I should be able to ignore her without worrying about hurting her feelings. I'd like an older woman who knows everything. Yes, maybe I'm looking for a substitute mother, but so what? If you think about it, that's really the ideal type. Anyway, in my position, I can have whatever kind of secretary I choose.

I don't like being the bad guy, so I didn't fire her personally; that's what assistants are for. I can't believe she'd call me at home to talk about it. Didn't she think I had considered all the factors? I resent her for confronting me with her needs. I'm sure lots of people would like this job; just because she wants it doesn't mean she's the right person for it. She shouldn't have put me in the position of having to justify my decision.

Although this woman didn't like her boss or the situation any better after doing this exercise, her attitude had changed. Through reconstructing her boss's feelings and needs, she could accept that it was a simple, irreconcilable conflict: not only wasn't she the kind of secretary he wanted, he wasn't the kind of boss she wanted. His assessment of her was accurate and she realized she needed to work for someone who would appreciate her ambition and enthusiasm. She let go of her resentment toward him and was able to rechannel her energy; instead of trying to hold onto the job, she began looking for another one both inside and outside the agency. Most of her anger had dissipated, so her search wasn't tinged with bitterness. It didn't take long to find a more gratifying position . . . one in which she could exercise more authority and creative thinking. She was given more responsibility and her new boss allowed her to try her hand at copy writing. She couldn't help being pleased that at the time of her departure her boss, who had inexplicably added fluent Portuguese to his list of secretarial requirements, still hadn't found a replacement.

She learned a vital lesson from this experience. She had known right from the start that she wasn't what he had wanted, but she had thought she could compensate for the discrepancies by working extra hard. She found out that life doesn't always work that way. As she expressed it, "If someone wants a chocolate sundae, and you're a vanilla sundae, it doesn't matter how much whipped cream, nuts, and cherries you put on yourself, you still won't be the chocolate sundae they want!"

Exercise 24:
WRITE A DREAM THAT EXPRESSES THE TROUBLING SITUATION OR EMOTION

You can also work with problems by writing a "dream" that expresses the troubling situation or emotion, and then doing a dreamwork exercise with it. In the process of constructing the "dream," previously hidden aspects of the problem can emerge and be explored; also the "dream" itself will distance you from the problem so that you can perceive it more objectively.

There are no rules or guidelines to follow in creating a dream; that's why it's so invaluable. Use this freedom from the restrictions and conventions of reality to fashion a story or series of images that best expresses the essence of what you want to examine. Open up your mind, rid yourself of preconceptions, and let your imagination run wild; this is a dream and anything can happen. Let it flow out of you. After you've written your "dream", use one or more dreamwork techniques with it.

A stock broker discovered the solution to his problem through this technique. After saving for many years, he bought a commercial building. Soon after, while it was being renovated, the building was nearly destroyed by flooding. Much of the city where his building is situated is built on marshland near a river along the mid-Atlantic coast; sometimes parts of the city sink, and severe flooding takes place. The city's sewer system is antiquated and in great disrepair, but the city won't fix it. It's an admittedly expensive job, but it has to be done. The stock broker was terribly worried that a major storm would totally demolish his building. He was reluctant to pressure the city however, because it is controlled by organized crime members who have been known to permanently silence loud complainers. This is how he described his feelings about the situation: "It's like having a wonderful dream materialize and then, when you approach it, it turns to shit." He expressed his problem in the following "dream."

My New Building

I gaze into my small, beautiful pond, watching the reflections of the sky, clouds, and surrounding flowers. Suddenly the pond begins to bubble, gurgle, foam and fume. The water level rises and spews forth shit and mud. Clouds form above. The water surrounds me, and I'm covered with all the dregs and mess of humanity, the by-products of all the evil doings in the world.

The filthy, foaming water surrounds and absorbs everything. It starts to erode the trees, and everything else crumbles and melts away. I'm encompassed in this muck and I can't swim. I struggle and people help me. Finally I climb to the top of a surviving tree and stay there as the water recedes. When I climb down from the tree I have to wend my way through the residues of hell that erupted from below; it's like demon matter.

I start cleaning the mess away, trying to turn it back into a pretty little pond. Then the pond

begins to rise up and bubble and spew shit again.
I realize that soon I might not find any more
trees to climb. It's an endless cycle. I struggle to
survive this bubbling cauldron of muck, but
every time it's subdued it rises up again.

The man used the dreamwork method of rewriting the
ending of the dream, giving it a positive resolution. This
technique can result in a new outcome to your problem-
atic situation as well as an enhanced sense of power in
your waking state.

My New Building (rewriting the ending)

All the other people join me and we get a huge
cement mixer, bigger than the city itself, and take
it to the pond, where it vomits out tons of concrete. The pond tries to fight back by spewing
out muck and other demon matter, but the cement is stronger. It seals up all the pores of this
evil force that's inundating everything with shit.
When it's finished there is no grass left, but the
trees are still growing, the sky is blue, and the
muck is gone forever.

The image of the huge cement mixer was the catalyst to
discovering the solution to his problem. He realized there
were probably many other people just as concerned and
yet equally afraid of organized crime. If they banded together, however, they could create a structure big enough
to take on the city and the mob. He talked to others in
the community, found that they did indeed share his feelings, and together they all filed a class action suit against
the city to force it to repair the sewer system. The case is
still in the courts, but the group feels optimistic because

their lawyer filed a similar suit against a neighboring city and won.

A woman wrote this "dream" about her inability to sustain a romantic relationship:

> **Trying to Find My Lover**
> I am at a resort-like motel, a sprawling complex, that's on the ocean. I'm trying to find my lover. I go from room to room looking for him. The rooms are filled with masses of people. When I do find him he disappears, and I have to look for him again.

She decided to try the free-association method on her "dream." This method consists of taking the pithiest paragraph from a written dream, listing in a column on the left-hand side of the page every single word in the paragraph as it appears, and free associating to each word in a column on the right. The dreamer then rewrites the paragraph using only the words in the right-hand column.

Trying to Find My Lover (free association)

am	exist, alive
resort	fun, free from care
motel	traveling, place for sex
sprawling	legs apart
complex	too many things, can be insidious
ocean	source of life, dangerous beauty
trying	hoping, might fail
find	catch, entrap, ensnare
my	part of me
lover	love object, most important, always out of reach
go	travel, move

room	possibility
looking	anxious, am without, want and need
filled	room for no more
masses	formless shapes, blobs
people	are they good or bad
disappears	gone forever, I'm left empty
have to	must, life depends on it
again	repeat, a cycle

After associating to each word, she rewrote the "dream" using just the associations.

Trying to Find My Lover (rewritten)

I exist alive at a fun, free from care, traveling, place for sex, legs apart too many things can be insidious, that's on the source of life, dangerous beauty. I exist hoping, might fail, to catch, entrap, ensnare out of my reach. I travel from possibility to possibility anxious, am without, want and need, always out of my reach. The possibilities are room for no more with formless shapes, blobs, are they good or bad. When I ensnare love object, always out of reach gone forever, I'm left empty, and part of my life depends on it, anxious for most important repeat, a cycle.

The woman gained important insights into the feelings that were sabotaging her ability to have a relationship. Her fears and ambivalence toward sexual relationships were revealed. She became aware that she was looking for a lover who could fill in the missing gaps in her, someone she could use to make herself whole. In her desperation, she would resort to any means, good or bad, to capture the person. Most surprising to her was the revelation that she didn't want the love object once she snared it. She felt empty because her real satisfaction came from the quest for something out of her reach, something safe. She had an emotional investment in ensuring that her relationships didn't last so that she could continue her cycle. This pattern was apparent in other areas of her life too: in her search for a career, in her initial enthusiasm at starting projects that quickly turned to disappointment. Once she became aware of her self-defeating tendency, she began making an effort to maintain her interest in the people and the activities in her life that had value for her.

You can use almost any dreamwork technique with waking-life problems. If you haven't yet found yourself in any of the examples so far, you're bound to identify with those that follow. Here is a powerful technique to bring up buried memories and provide insights.

Exercise 25:
THE MYTH–FAIRY TALE METHOD

Personal myths are the source of many of our assumptions about life and ourselves; they are our earliest memories of the key events that formed or altered our perceptions of the world. Noted humanist psychologist Stanley Krippner said of myths: "Myths can be helpful; myths can be harmful. Myths can be creative; myths can be destructive. Yet myths were indispensable in earlier times because they supplied a retrospective pattern of moral values, sociological order and magical belief. Thus they fulfilled a function closely connected with the nature of tradition, with the continuity of culture, with the relation between youth and age, and with humans' attitudes toward the past. Our mythic underworld can still help us to clarify our values, make sense of our social roles, and bring a sense of wonder to the world around us."[12]

Krippner added that personal myths are guides and paths to self-healing that are revealed to us in our fantasies and dreams.

Krippner uses a powerful technique for working with dreams that I have applied to waking-life problems. The exercise entails discovering your personal myth via the fairy tale and is composed of several steps. You will probably want to read all of them before beginning the exercise. These are the steps:

1. Recall a waking-life situation that is disturbing and unresolved. What is the primary emotion? With your eyes closed and your body in a relaxed position, feel that emotion in your body, and notice where and how it manifests itself. Then recall the earliest childhood or adolescent incident in which you felt this emotion. Give yourself all the time you need to experience this fully.

2. Now imagine the emotion that is the opposite of the first one, and feel it also in your body. Allowing yourself ample time to experience it fully, recall your earliest memory of this feeling.

3. Now write these incidents as a fairy tale, as in "once upon a time there was a little girl—or boy. . . ." Writing the incident in the third person gives you a different perspective on it and opens up new areas to explore. It may feel as if someone else inside of you is writing your story, exposing incidents and truths you never imagined.

Chapter One of the fairy tale below recreates the first childhood incident in story form. Chapter Two depicts the second and counterpoint incident, also in story form. Even if the two incidents are separated by many years, allow Chapter One to flow into Chapter Two in story-like fashion.

4. Lie down, close your eyes again, and imagine holding the first incident (myth) in one hand and the second incident (myth) in the other; it doesn't matter which hand you choose. Feel each myth as a physical sensation, and ascribe an image to each sensation. Imagine these two images coming together. Do they remain separate? Does one dominate? Do they change each other? Write what happens when these two images meet. This is Chapter Three of the fairy tale, the resolution.

Gary, the man who wrote the fairy tale that follows, spent his whole life trying to avoid being hurt by others:

Avoidance of Pain

Chapter One

Once upon a time there was a little boy named Gary who lived with his mother, father, and sister. Gary's father was a doctor, and one Sunday every summer his aunts, uncles, and cousins would come over to the house so that Gary's father could give all the children their shots for camp.

Nothing in the world frightened Gary more than the thought of getting a needle. The mere mention of it terrified him. He felt the pain would destroy him, and he fought against the needle as if his life depended on it. His parents always tried to give him as little advance warning as possible because it upset him so, but he invariably got wind of it days ahead of time and badgered them with tearful questions about the date of that terrible day. As soon as his fears were confirmed, the hysteria began. He alternated between forcefully asserting that there was no way he was going to get the shot, to screaming, pleading, and writhing on the floor.

The day of the shot invariably found Gary desperately

trying every possible emotional ploy to avoid it. His temperature rose two or three degrees and he'd barricade himself in his room. His family always dreaded this day, and his relatives were embarrassed and bewildered; they all knew Gary would create a terrible scene. One by one, the others entered the kitchen and Gary's father gave them their shots. Gary was always last; his mother fed him aspirin to make his fever go down. Gary hysterically pleaded with them, giving everything he had to try to convince them not to do this thing to him that he couldn't endure. It never worked.

Of course, Gary always survived. When it was his turn his mother led him into the kitchen and held him down while his father gave him the needle. It hurt but he didn't die. He was always in such a state of shock and terror though that he never realized that it didn't kill him. He was very upset that no one listened to him when he said he couldn't handle it. He invariably lost his battle to protect himself, and felt powerless and helpless. In this way, the excruciating agony of failing to avoid the shot (which he experienced as death) was inextricably linked to the negligible pain of the shot itself.

Chapter Two

Then one day Gary went to his first boy-girl party. Everyone was dancing the Twist to Chubby Checker records. Gary loved to dance and started showing off. He watched "American Bandstand" and could do all sorts of fancy steps. He was lowering himself down to the floor as he did the Twist, seeing how far he could go, when he slipped and fell. There was a loud crack. Gary was on the floor, and his left kneecap was on the side of his leg instead of on the top. Everyone rushed all around him, and the parents of the birthday girl called an ambulance. Gary was very brave, making jokes and downplaying the whole thing. After all, he was an equestrian and wasn't afraid of pain. To show off his bravery and mastery over the situation, he made a fist and banged his knee back into place by himself. All the girls screamed and even the boys looked pale as his knee clicked back into place. It hurt a lot when he did it, more than he thought it would, but he didn't show his pain or his fear. His knee quickly swelled up very big. He was carried to the ambulance on a stretcher, telling jokes the whole time.

Gary then did the last part of the exercise, which consisted of lying down on the floor, closing his eyes, and imagining holding the first incident in one hand and the second incident in the other. In his right hand he held the desperation and fear connected with trying to avoid pain; it felt like frantic, unsuccessful attempts to jerk his hand away from something. He created the terrifying image of being tied down to a conveyor belt heading for a chainsaw. In his left hand he held his nonavoidance of pain; it felt heavy and strong. He envisioned a large, solid, iron cube. He brought the two images together, and wrote the outcome as Chapter Three of the fairy tale.

Chapter Three

I bring together the image of me helplessly heading for the chainsaw and the image of the iron cube. The cube falls between me and the chainsaw, saving me from it. The teeth of the saw grind against the cube until they are worn down.

Gary realized that there was a protective barrier between him and unbearable pain, and it was strong enough to safeguard even his most vulnerable areas. He didn't have to spend his life trying to avoid pain. While writing Chapter One, he also became aware that his fear of pain was usually more agonizing than the actual pain he was trying to avoid. As a result, he began to take more chances in his life: went to more social gatherings, asked more women for dates, spoke up at his political club meetings. He even took up skiing, a sport he had always wanted to try but hadn't done so for fear of injuring himself. Gradually he was able to experience emotional distress without worrying that it would destroy him.

The insights people gain from doing this exercise are often quite amazing. Only by doing the exercise yourself can you fully understand this.

A young woman thought her problem was always wanting things her own way and wrote the following fairy tale:

Not Getting Things the Way I Want Them

Chapter One

Once upon a time there was a little girl named Betty. She wanted a certain kind of doll, called a "troll," that was currently all the rage. Everyone at her school had one and she begged her mother to buy her one.

The following day, Betty's mother came home with a troll doll and gave it to her. Betty was devastated; it wasn't the original, "right" brand, but rather another company's copy of it. Her mother couldn't tell the difference, of course, but Betty and all her friends could. Betty said nothing about this to her mother; she was very concerned about hurting her mother's feelings because her mother had been happy to buy it for her. Betty went into her bedroom and sobbed. She didn't like the doll. She felt terribly guilty for not appreciating her mother's gift and hated herself because she couldn't love the doll since it was the wrong kind. She thought she was an awful person and vowed to hide her feelings from her mother so her mother wouldn't be hurt. She thought her mother would be crushed if she knew the truth.

Chapter Two

Betty loved to stay home when she was sick with a cold, because she got exactly what she wanted. She didn't have to go to school and didn't have to share her mother with her brothers. Her mother would make a cozy bed for her on the couch in the den, and she could watch the afternoon movies on television and read. Best of all, her mother would let her drink hot tea with lemon, which Betty considered a grown-up drink. Her mother would play with her, and Betty felt totally protected and safe from the cruelties of the outside world. It was perfect, and she wanted it to remain that way forever.

In her right hand, Betty held the sensation of not getting what she wanted in the right way. Her hand felt as if it were being brutally stabbed, and she pictured razor-sharp knives. In her left hand was perfection, getting something just the way she wanted it. It felt soft, round, and firm, like a pincushion. She wrote Chapter Three about the meeting of these two images.

Chapter Three

The knives and the pincushion are brought together. The knives pierce the pincushion and tear it apart. Its insides come out and it falls to pieces.

Betty received two important messages from this exercise. Before doing this exercise, she had thought her problem was wanting things her own way. She now realized that while there was nothing intrinsically wrong with wanting to be satisfied in the way she desired, her standards entailed an often unattainable degree of perfection and safety. As long as her desires were so narrow and unrealistic, she frequently suffered the pain of disappointment. She had to broaden her expectations so that her needs could be satisfied more often. She also became aware of her rigidity in perceiving satisfaction. To her it was all or nothing. If something didn't fulfill her desires in the exact form she demanded, it was worthless to her and tantamount to receiving nothing. Because she perceived no middle ground and had no flexibility, she was unable to accept and appreciate much of the value that was being offered to her because the form did not measure up to her standards.

This pattern also extended to her wish to write—a wish that never materialized because she'd begin comparing herself to the great names in literature. After doing this exercise, she picked up the pen and struggled to continue writing even through her self-negations. "I'm not Katherine Mansfield," she'd say, "but I AM *me*." She's now writing short stories.

Ruth suffered from intense feelings of abandonment all her life. Recently she experienced them during a bitter argument with her husband. She wrote the following fairy tale:

Being Abandoned

Chapter One

Once upon a time there was a little girl named Ruth who lived with her mother, father, and her governess Anna. Anna had been with the little girl ever since she was born, which was about five years ago, and Ruth loved her deeply. In some ways Ruth was closer to Anna than she was to her mother. Anna would go away over the weekends, but she always came back on Monday. One Friday Anna said goodbye to the little girl. Ruth was very busy playing and so didn't pay much attention to her.

On Sunday, Ruth's mother told her that Anna wasn't coming back; she was going to live with her own children. Ruth was very unhappy and screamed and cried. Why did Anna want to be with her own children and not her? Why hadn't Anna told her she was leaving and said goodbye? Her mother said that Anna wanted to retire, and that she and Anna had decided it would be better not to tell Ruth beforehand so that she wouldn't get upset. Ruth was devastated, angry and sad. She missed Anna terribly and felt that a huge chunk of her insides had been torn out. She felt all alone, and couldn't believe Anna was gone.

Two weeks later, Anna came to visit for the day. Anna tried to talk to the little girl, to tell her that she loved her. But Ruth was so angry and hurt that she pretended she didn't know who Anna was, and wouldn't talk to her. It hurt Ruth terribly to do this, but she thought it would protect her from the worse pain of acknowledging Anna and feeling love for her while at the same time confronting the fact that Anna had suddenly abandoned her, without warning, for someone else. The little girl assumed, trusted, that Anna would know that she was mad and would come back and try to make up with her again. So she never stopped acting like she didn't know Anna. Anna was sad and finally left.

Anna never came back, and Ruth never saw or heard from her again. The little girl lost more than Anna. She lost her sense of security that the people she loved wouldn't disappear without warning. She lost her feeling of being a special and lovable person who people would struggle and fight to remain close to; instead she thought that there was something (she didn't know what) intrinsically unlovable about her, and that it was very easy for people to leave her and find someone better, and never think of her again. She hated herself for being mean to Anna when Anna came to visit; maybe if she hadn't shown her anger Anna would have stayed. She began to think it wasn't safe to show anger toward people she loved. She blamed herself for Anna leaving, and was frightened by how easy it was for her to drive people away forever.

Chapter Two

The summer before her fourteenth birthday, Ruth went to music camp. She was one of the youngest people there; most of the others were fifteen to seventeen. The people there shared her interest in music and philosophy, and she became very close to a group of them. This was in the late 1960s, and everyone was very demonstrative about their love for the others. The relationships were intense. While misunderstandings sometimes occurred, Ruth felt truly loved for the first time since Anna left. She felt secure that no matter what might arise between her and her friends, her friends would never leave her or let her go; they would do everything possible to resolve the problem. She was that important to them. Ruth was happier than she had ever been in her whole life; she lost some of her sense of being unlovable and easily abandoned.

Ruth held the feeling of being abandoned in her right hand; it was devastation and death and she came up with the image of an endless black void. In her left hand she felt the security of being loved; it was smooth, hard, solid, like a mirror. She brought the two together.

Chapter Three

Ruth brought the mirror and the void together; the mirror reflected the void so that it looked like she had a void in both hands. However, she could still feel the mirror even though she couldn't see it.

From doing this exercise, Ruth realized that much of her sense of unlovability and abandonment was her own invention; in reality, that wasn't what people felt for her. But the way she constructed it, she couldn't see anything else. She now knew she would have to develop other tools, just as she had used her sense of touch to feel the mirror when she couldn't see it. With this newfound sense of security, she was willing to risk more in intimate situations. Instead of shouting at her husband because he didn't give her what she wanted, she began to assertively tell him what she wanted. And he was better able to respond. The memory of the music camp convinced her to play the piano again. And she talked her husband into buying her a piano.

Re-creating your own personal myth through fairy tales is a strong and revealing method for unmasking and examining your assumptions about yourself and the world, and for releasing your creativity. The individuals cited in this chapter saw the underlying dynamics of their problems for the first time, and these insights freed their energy for creative expression. The more you understand and utilize the connection between your waking life and your unconscious, the more fulfilling your life will be.

10

THE MIRACLES THAT HAPPEN IN GROUPS

A creativity group has certain advantages that no other interaction can offer. The feedback you will receive in a group is invaluable. The interchange with people from different backgrounds and life experiences can expose you to unexpected points of view and, in turn, significantly broaden your outlook. The insights are sometimes mind-boggling, especially when all the members of the group are engaged in heightening their creativity.

Creativity groups vary in their themes and structures. In my eight-week dreamwork workshop for creative people I combined two techniques that would unearth the seeds of creativity during waking hours and utilize dreams at night for further discovery. This method was experimental and proved effective because the daywork enhanced the nightwork and vice versa. At night the group members practiced the incubation technique of asking their dream for a solution to a creative problem (see Chapter Five). During the daytime workshop they participated in a modified version of the Montague Ullman dream method, which will be described below. Montague Ullman is a prominent psychiatrist known for his work with dreams. The Ullman method worked to trigger immediate connections and interactions among group members.

The results at times were stunning—not only the insights during the workshop itself, but people actualizing in their lives what they'd been looking for in their dreams. The process is not a conscious one but simply "happens," because the unconscious has been activated. A woman exclaimed two months after a workshop: "I don't know how or why, but these exercises have affected my subconscious. My energy has zoomed." Why these changes take place may become clear as you read the excerpts of the group in process. I have disguised identities and greatly condensed the content to best illustrate the process.

First, let's meet the members of the group. Ben, a college administrator, wants to unblock himself as a painter; he is interested in painting the figure but is not sure how to approach his subject matter. Anne is a painter who wants to fulfill herself more completely as an artist. She works as a teacher to help support her family and does not have the time she needs to paint.

George, an engineer, wants to be a more creative photographer. Sarah, an actress, wants to deal with her stage fright and fear of people. Ginny, a set designer, confessed, "My work consumes me; I want to rediscover who I am." Patricia, a high school teacher, has not yet found what she is looking for. Charlotte, a gallery owner, wants to discover her creativity again, which has become lost in the business aspects of her work. Mark, a historian, wants support in writing his new book and the inner resources to trust himself as a writer and speaker. He is still grieving the loss of his wife, who died last year. Seth, a financial analyst, admits, "I don't know what I want to do, in work and in other areas of my life." And Don, a church rector, comments, "I have all these things inside of me that I want to express, but I don't know how to access them."

As the workshop proceeded, each of these people made important discoveries. For the sake of clarity, I have focused on only four members of the group. In this way you will be able to trace their process and their progress from week to week.

The participants agreed to tell their dreams at the beginning of each session of the workshop. Some of the participants offered their dreams to the group for work in depth. The dream work was so intensive that there was usually only time for one dream per meeting. If more than one person felt an urgency to explore a dream, the group leader would flip a coin to decide. All the dreams came out of the weekly incubation technique: asking dreams for the solution to a creative problem. By the end of the eight weeks, each member had experienced the benefit of the group's input on at least one dream.

Exercise 26:
CREATING FROM ANOTHER'S DREAM

Here's how it works. The dreamer tells a dream. Each member jots down every detail of the chosen dream. Each person then tells the dream as if he or she actually dreamt it, including all associations to the dream, interpretations and commentary on what the dream means. Each time a new "dreamer" tells the dream, he or she makes it clear this is his or her dream. The initial dreamer sits back quietly and listens, taking note of anything that resonates or rings true. This part of the exercise is based on Montague Ullman's dreamwork method. My addition to this technique is to ask each member of the group to write a vignette, story, poem, or play based on one or more of the dream elements; or make a painting or drawing; or create anything whatsoever that is based on the dream that is told during that day's group session. Group members do this at home.

Why ask group members to create from someone else's dream rather than from their own? Working from someone else's material provides a safe distance from the content in one's own life that might be too difficult or too painful to handle. It also frees the person from self-consciousness. We all have a tendency to gravitate toward that aspect of someone else's dream that has meaning for us; what we chose is not by chance! And it is the very distance from our own material that enables us to open ourselves to sometimes very profound experiences.

The members of the group also did the incubation exercise described in Chapter Five every night of the week just as they were falling asleep. They reflected upon a creative issue of their own, and then formulated a clear, succinct question for their unconscious to answer. They repeated this question over and over again to themselves until they dozed off. Then, they asked their dreams probing questions about their own creativity and how to get what they wanted. At the beginning of each session they discussed creative insights, dreams, or events during the week. My job was mainly as a facilitator. I will present here just the highlights of the sessions, focusing on the content of four members: Ginny, Ben, Anne, and Mark.

FIRST WEEK

During the first meeting, Ginny presented her dream. Ginny, as you may remember, was a set designer whose career was consuming all of her time. She felt that her "self" had become lost in the shuffle, and she wanted to rediscover herself. After she presented her dream to the group, they did the Ullman method with it. This is Ginny's dream:

> I find myself on a beach. It's a clear day, the ocean is calm, and there are two or three small clouds in the sky. A few minutes later I notice the clouds are not moving in the same way as they are being reflected by the waves and the sand. On the right, I am aware of Jim, my ex-lover, wrestling with green foam rubber in the shape of Italy, the boot. And he's making these hills of Rome out of the foam rubber. It strikes me as odd. I ask him what he's doing. He says, "I have to do this so that I know what I'm doing"—something which seemed totally sense-less at the time. I say, "I'll help you." Eventually we end up in what appears to be a very realistic bedroom, but one we have never been in. The telephone rings and he has a conversation with his brother. He says, "Ginny is here, and we're making stuff. We're having a lot of fun. We're going to keep making stuff and making stuff."

After Ginny told the dream, and everyone took a turn telling it as if it were his or her own, Ginny explained that

Jim was "the man I broke up with twice—it's still unresolved." Then she brought up a related topic: "I made this decision to totally decorate my home. I'm 33 years old. When am I going to do it? That has become my creative challenge. Even though I spend my life setting the stage, finding the perfect prop, painting the most beautiful room, I've never done that for *me*. I never set *my* stage. It has become really important to me."

SECOND WEEK

The group members were anxious to share the dreams they had had during the week. They told their dreams and Ben, the college administrator who wanted to paint the figure, offered his dream for group work. Before we attend to Ben's dream, let's look at the dreams of the three others whose processes will follow. Mark, the historian who was writing his book and speaking in public, prefaced his dream by saying,

> "During the week, I was thinking about some core issues: I had wanted to be a concert pianist when I was a child. That had to be submerged. My family discouraged me from enjoying anything pleasurable, anything that wasn't work. They did not want me to pursue my interests. If I did, I'd be interrupted. The way my family dealt with this could relate to problems I am having now with writing my book and speaking publicly. I thought about these issues before going to sleep and had this dream:

"I am at a party, and I walk out the door. Suddenly I am in an Alice-in-Wonderland setting that is all wilderness and forest. A buffalo starts coming toward me. I'm standing on the threshold of the apartment and my student is there. I want him to help me close the door so that the buffalo doesn't get in. He doesn't cooperate. The buffalo comes through the door and runs me over . . . although I don't think I am hurt.

"After the dream I asked myself the question: 'What is the buffalo doing in my dream?' And I started singing 'Home, Home on the Range.' The words to this song are very interesting: 'Oh give me a home where the buffalo roam and the deer and the antelope play. Where seldom is heard a discouraging word and the skies are not cloudy all day.' It was a vision for a very pleasant nurturing supportive environment. I've been singing this song all week. Yet it's not one of my favorite songs. I often will think of lyrics of songs to express emotions. Later in the week I had another dream that related to the buffalo dream. In this dream:

"I am at a seminar. There is a colleague in the audience whom I recognize, and who, during the entire course of the evening, never nods in my direction. It is someone I worked with a couple of years ago, and I'm sure he knows me. And I am mad at him all night long for not speaking to me. I see him avoiding my eyes, and I begin to feel a constriction in my throat. I am sure he is purposely ignoring me. And I am developing this whole anger at his arrogance.

"My associations to the dream were that the colleague was competitive with me. I knew that the buffalo had something to do with this man. It hadn't occurred to me that both the colleague and the buffalo represented my older brother. Also my brother's initials are B.B.—as in 'Buffalo Bill.' That was the kind of relationship I had with my brother. He was always competing with me and was jealous because I have always been more successful than him."

Anne, who wanted more fulfillment as a painter, told the following dream:

"The scene is a multi-tiered beautiful loft space . . . with modern furnishings and a warm golden woody look. A man and a huge ape wrestle with each other, moving from the first to the second to the third levels, using a stairwell that's cut in tiered drawer-like shelves in a larger space. They fight with concentration, determination, glaring at each other. There is a calculated pause between each physical encounter. They roll around on the floor, falling and climbing to different levels as the fight proceeds. They separate and re-engage, glaring at each other while apart. I become the man. I am glaring into the eyes of the beast. I seem to be looking into a very familiar pair of enraged eyes. I know the beast very well.

> The encounter ceases. The beast is subdued.
> He lies against the wall. Other people ap-
> pear. The beast moves to avoid confronta-
> tion, and retreats. As he is leaving, I invite
> him pleadingly to have something to eat.
> 'Oh won't you stay and have dinner with
> us.' He goes away. I am sad to see him go.

"As I was telling this dream," Anne told the group, "it
dawned on me, *the beast was my chairman*! [Anne teaches
in the art department of a high school.]

> "At first, I thought the beast represented the cre-
> ative part of me that's trying to break free. And
> I'm subduing it. I put down that creative part of
> me. Of course, this is true too. But then when I
> see it disappear and go away, I'm really sorry to
> see it go. I also have similar feelings towards my
> chairman. I've worked for him for many many
> years. He was a friend before I worked for him.
> So I don't completely hate this man. I'm having
> a very difficult time with him now. One part of
> me feels I'm in an untenable position, but an-
> other part says, 'You're a jerk. Why do you take
> these things?' I really have to clear the air and
> talk to him about my feelings and what's going
> on."

One of the group's rules is that no one is to comment
upon someone else's dream until that dream becomes the
"group dream" and benefits from the group process. Ad-
herence to this rule is crucial to the dreamer developing
a sense of trust. The purpose of the work is to enable the
dreamer to reach an understanding of the dream through
the group providing an atmosphere that will draw out

further associations from the dreamer. Each person (other than the dreamer) tells the dream as if it is his or her own. Because many of our thoughts and feelings are universal, people inadvertently say things that may resonate truths for the dreamer. But no one is allowed to interpret because that can mislead the dreamer from his or her own inner truth. The interpretation is usually a projection of the person making it anyway. Each dream is a unique creation of that particular dreamer and is related to that dreamer's life experience and psychology.

However, since I had the opportunity of witnessing Anne's process throughout the eight weeks, I offer here an interpretation to help you, the reader, follow the process.

The beast, as I see it, represents both the creative part of Anne and her chairman as well. A part of her is at war with each of them, but it is her chairman that is *also* stifling her creativity. She likes him and is afraid he will be hurt if she confronts him. Dreams can have multiple meanings.

Ginny, who keeps dreaming about Jim and also trying to get her life together, told the group:

> "The burning creative question in my mind that I asked of my dream was, 'How am I going to organize this work space to make it work for me—and to be able to rent it out?' It's an important creative problem to me. When I woke up in the morning, I had no memory of what I dreamt, except the very last fragment. In this fragment, I was sitting next to a child's red wagon with Jim, and he said, 'I'll help you, I'll help you put up the shelves. We'll get it done together.' And then I woke up, and I thought, 'Another Jim dream. Is this a wish dream?'

"Later that same morning I went into a garden store, and I got into a conversation with the guy behind the counter, but somehow I mentioned that I wanted to get a child's wagon to help me with my work. And he said, 'No problem. There's a place out in Jersey. I can get it for you wholesale.' So we went about arranging that.

"Then the dream changed direction. When I got home, I got my courage to call Jim's brother who is very supportive of me as an artist. I needed to talk to him, and he wanted to come and help me. And he said, 'You really have to call Jim. He really misses you. He needs to talk to you. This would be very good for him.'

"I still haven't called Jim, but because of the dream I thought of at least calling his brother. The dream inspired me in some way to just go about doing these small things to get what I want and to solve my workspace problem . . . When I first met Jim I was a student. And I now have totally changed my life. Not because he said to, but just because of his atmosphere—whatever we did together, whatever we created together."

It became more and more apparent that the presence of Jim in her dreams inspired Ginny's creativity. She held him in her mind as she carried out her goals by herself. Jim functioned inside of her almost as a muse. Creative inspiration can be linked to the loved one.

The group had selected Ben's dream for that evening and applied Montague Ullman's technique to it. You will see how some of the other people in the group were able to make Ben's dream their own. Ben had reached an impasse in his painting and was not sure of how to approach his subject matter. Ben's dream:

I am on a ship. It isn't an ocean liner; it is an aircraft carrier. I am standing on the deck. It is quite small and there is an object coming up above the deck with a mast of some sort. The ship is in danger. I think there may have been a storm. The ship cracks in two. And there are other people on the ship. I don't see them, but I know they are there. I realize that the front part of the ship is safe. It is either attached to land or it is not going to sink. But the part of the ship that I am on is going to sink.

I can see that this part of the ship is trying to connect to the front of the boat. It is like a train hook-up. And the part of the ship that I am on has come close to the other one and almost connects, but doesn't quite make it. I realize that this boat is going to sink and I am going to drown, but I also realize that I may be able to leap onto the other part of the ship, the safe part, and save myself. And at some point I take a big jump and land on the safe front part of the ship. I am standing on this part, and I suddenly feel as if I have done something wrong. The people on the other side of the boat are drowning. So I jump back on to the sinking part. The boat sinks and I drown.

I know what I look like in the dream drowning. I am rolled up like a ball. Then I know that I am dreaming. In the dream I say to myself, 'You can't dream that you have died.' But I am surprised in the dream to discover I am dead. And I am also very surprised that I don't mind. The part of the boat that is safe comes to a point, but the part of the boat that I am on has a hole. It fits together because the hole fits over the cone.

Anne volunteered to tell the dream next. This is her version:

> "When I had this dream, the ship was my body. There are two parts of my body. I have a male side and I have a female side.[13] I'm weak and I wish I could be stronger. I wish I could jump to the male side and survive, and go ahead and go forth and be assertive. But I can't. My nature is to be feminine and receptive, and I will plumb those depths of my nature. And I will sink into that part of myself."

Ginny's version was as follows:

> "In my dream, this ship is a very hospitable place for things to land on. It's a very strong place. It can take a lot. Unfortunately circumstances are such that this strong ship is struck by storms and war. And I am very shook up by it. Because the parts of my personality—the male part, the aggressive assertive part, and the female part, although just as strong—are separated in the course of this turmoil. And I'm very ambivalent as to what to do. I find myself playing a role of staying with the so-called female part of my body and de-

nying the part that can survive and continue on.''

Mark retold Ben's dream this way:

"I had a dream that I was out on this ship,
and I wanted to be free, happy, have a good
time, and be successful. But I felt very alone
and scared. I felt out of contact with other
people. I felt guilty. I was worried that I was
in danger—that something would happen
to me. I was horrified when the boat began
to break apart. My worst fears were coming
true. I was going to die alone. I knew I had
to save myself, and I looked around for a
way to do it. I knew I had to survive. I was
too frightened to leap to the other side of
the ship for fear I would not make it and I
would wind up falling in the water and
drowning. So I knew I had to do something.
I finally took the chance and leapt to the
other side. At first I was happy I had been
able to survive. And then I was again overcome with feeling alone and terribly guilty.
So I jumped back to the sinking part of the
boat, which meant to me that I would die.
I felt too pulled by my own aloneness and
my own feelings of guilt to really let myself
succeed."

As you see, by telling the dream, each person reveals a
compelling concern of his or her own, and is not focussing
on Ben at all. Anne feels she is not able to survive in a
crisis because she is a woman and therefore weak. Ginny,
too, although she feels both her female and male sides are

equally strong, denies the male part of herself, the part that could save her. Mark, who longs to feel free, joyous, and successful, experiences loneliness and guilt instead. He must put others first, save himself last, or he will be abandoned emotionally.

So by telling their dream as if it were their own, they all get in touch with their own issues. They also give information to Ben about the underlying meaning of his dream. Some of the themes covered in this dream have to do with male–female traits and what the dreamers consider strong or weak. There is also the motif of putting others before one's own survival for fear of being abandoned.

THIRD WEEK

The workshop began with Anne showing the group her drawing of a dream she had had the first week of the workshop. In the drawing she is a bug sitting in green grass. In the dream she's told, "Carry what you're capable of carrying—not more, not less—and you'll be happy." About the drawing, she said, "It's a breakthrough in my style. Normally I'd draw a bug realistically, as a graphic artist might. But this drawing is abstract—the shape that the grass makes, the two-dimensionality, and the unrealistic color. This is more like fine art."

She then brought out a collage and said,

> "I also had another breakthrough. I did a collage based on Ben's dream last week; in it I am trying to unite my masculine and feminine selves. As I was working, I saw that I had more than two

selves. And I realized that is one of the main problems in my life—these shattered selves. I feel I'm being pulled in different directions. I did some simple collages during the week, but then I remembered that this theme recurs in my work. I brought in two etchings that relate to this subject. And I brought in the collages that I did during the week. I felt Ben's dream could have been my dream. This is me. I'm always running here and running there, and going with this one, and not spending time with myself and not doing the things that are important to me. And it's my choice that I'm making. I'm not blaming it on anyone else. I'm choosing to sabotage myself, and it really came out in the exercise. I saw the ship as my body and the two parts being separated—and trying to bring the parts of my personality more in harmony. And not succeeding . . ."

Ben spoke up and said that he had dreamt during the week about two purple ships colliding in the night (a variation on the boat theme). They had transformed into purple bookshelves and had merged, forming great wealths of knowledge. (It begins to make sense, especially as you read further, that Ben is beginning to look toward himself, not others, for insights.)

Ginny commented:

"Whenever I do recall my dreams, this character Jim is in them—to the point where that's beginning to get to me. The dreams themselves are usually very funny, so I wake in a good mood. In one of the dreams, for example, he and I are

in a restaurant where they are serving leftover
food because it is cheaper.

"On other mornings I didn't remember my
dreams but I know I had them. On those mornings, when I woke up I was very productive,
more productive."

Even though she didn't *remember* her dreams, they were
nevertheless affecting her. Although it is helpful to recall
a dream so that we may work on it while we're awake,
the unconscious can solve problems without our conscious awareness of it. The neurological process continues
even when we are sleeping.

Mark said to Ben:

"I was troubled by the way I ended your dream
last week. I would not have gone back to the
side of the ship that sank, but I would have felt
guilty for having survived. That was on my mind.
The next morning I woke up remembering a
book I had read 24 years ago. I climbed up to
find it on a high shelf, and I reread the chapter.
It was from Thomas Mann's *The Magic Mountain:*
the story of a man who seeks truth about life,
but is avoiding life at the same time. He goes out
into the snow and gets lost and can't find his
way home. He doesn't have the will to get back.
He falls asleep and has a beautiful dream, but it
ends with the sacrifice of a child. Through the
dream, the hero reaches his goal. He has dreamed
it out to the end: love over death, with the
knowledge of death there . . . . The first night of
this workshop, I had a dream at four A.M. about
a woman I knew in my fourth year of college

who killed herself. Right after it happened, I read this very chapter from Thomas Mann. In the first week of the dream workshop I did a written dialogue with the woman who killed herself. She said to me in the dialogue, 'Get on your soap box, Mark. Don't let anybody stop you.' I like this idea of leaving death behind to live life.''

Mark is tormented by survivor's guilt. His wife has died, and a part of him feels he has no right to live. This conflict brings forth from the unconscious forgotten events of the past that caused him to feel a similar way and that reappear in his dreams. The healthy part of him, of course, wishes to live.

FOURTH WEEK

This week the group members' dreaming life was beginning to enter into their waking life. There was not as much separation between the two. Anne, for example, who initially had been dissatisfied with the way her painting was going, reported:

"I saw a movie and later that night I formulated an incubation question that was based on this movie. The movie was *Field of Dreams*. There was a line in it that haunted me. The hero's father says, 'You only have your chance one day.' He had wanted to play baseball and didn't do it that day. He said, 'I always thought there'd be another day. I missed my chance. I never got what I wanted.' And that's the haunting thing with me. I'm getting older. I've missed my opportunity. I had a lot of golden opportunities when I was young to do a lot of interesting things, and I just didn't fulfill them. I thought always there's another day. That movie brought it out, how over and over again, I've missed my chance. Another day passed. It's too late.

"So I did the incubation technique. I asked my dream, 'Is it too late to take a chance?' And I had this dream before I woke up. It was very involved; there were a lot of people in it and a lot of things happening in it; it had everybody in my life in it. And it ended in a very symbolic way. I wrote it all down and then let it drop. I had no idea that it was answering my question. It didn't overtly say anything about it being too late. Not till later did I understand what it meant. This was my dream:

I'm teaching, and I threaten the kids to come back into the classroom; they are not doing what they are told. Everyone is staring at me. One of the kids tells me someone has a gun and is going to shoot me. I say, 'Okay, I'll go to heaven, you'll go to jail.' I find some scissors and realize it symbolizes my need to break away from the past.

In the next part, I'm signing up for classes. An old boyfriend of mine appears. He and I fantasize a lot in real life. I don't want him in my dream.

Then I'm at a control panel; I dim the lights and I feel frightened. I'm alone. Turning off the lights is saying goodbye to the past. I run out of my house but keep one light on. My sister knocks me down and I roll down a hill into bushes.

At the end of the dream, I'm walking down a road with a knapsack. It's a bright sunny day. I meet a beautiful woman also with a knapsack and we walk down the road together.

"Later when I was jogging, I thought, 'Just interpret the dream as you interpreted the movie.' As soon as I got home, I started writing. And it was like a game and it was really fun, because I didn't take it so personally—even though I felt the dream at first was saying something awful. But it ended up being the most incredibly uplifting dream: finding this beautiful woman also on the run and going off somewhere together. I realized she represents my higher self.

"I felt a lot of power from the images in the dream. And I suspected the power could be materialized, could be used if I could catch it and hold onto it and look at it and say, 'Ah-ah, that's it!' I started finding out everything imaginable about my life in this dream. I wrote ten pages. After that, I added a slash and wrote my interpretation of my life—of where I stood. I was able to bring out suppressed desires I've been having in my life and materialize them. But not consciously. For example, I love the color green and it comes up a lot in my dreams. Yet I'm not really conscious of it in my waking life. The day after I interpreted the dream I was running on this huge big green field. It was bright green and there was a baseball diamond. I hadn't told myself to go to the baseball field. I just happened to be there. I was running around this diamond all by myself. My family was way up by the tennis courts. I found a baseball and I began throwing it up in the air. It was as if I was hearing this message: 'Play the game. You can play the game. It's not too late to take a chance.' It made me feel very powerful, a feeling which I haven't felt before."

Anne was beginning to realize on an unconscious level that she needed to break away from certain past attachments to discover her aliveness and deep creativity.

Mark told the group:

"I used the incubation technique to ask my dreams: 'What's blocking my writing and what's my anxiety about speaking publicly?' I've had a lot of dreams on that thread. When I reread them I realized that one of the things I hadn't picked up on was my search for freedom, my search for fun, that was also going on, in addition to my feelings about being alone. I'm not supported in my intellectual work or creative activities. And I realized that when I was younger I was never allowed to read a book because that was viewed as not working. You were having fun, you weren't doing anything that was really productive. And I'm beginning for the first time to find a lot of pleasure in writing. I'm just really enjoying immersing myself in what I'm doing, and that's something I rarely do. And lately, speaking is a lot of fun, especially when people are appreciative. And so I am not having *only* the anxiety effect; it's a turn-on too. I'm letting my other responsibilities wait, like washing the car. I'm going to do my thing.''

Ginny reported on her dreams:

"Jim has been in every single one of my dreams. This morning I dreamt that Jim and I were sitting in a baby pool in my garden. I'm beginning to feel I should take the first step. Just do it, call him. I'm getting to be totally nuts. Maybe what's happening to me is I am beginning to live some of my dreams. I've realized a garden, I've realized a workspace. It's all really scary. I'm taking a whole lot of risks. I'm going to make it happen, damn it. Every day I'm doing something about it. I'll be in the garden tonight doing something. Maybe the dream world has gone into my real life. And I'm taking more chances, just going after it. Early on, I asked my dreams, 'How do I approach Jim?' Well, he's in every single dream and I'm approaching him in some other way, for example, 'Come sit in my garden pool,' or 'collect fish in a fish market.' I get that close to actually picking up the phone. One thing I've been realizing is that I'm entitled to have a life and not just get the leftovers, the hand-me-downs. My dreams are now coming into my life, which is very exciting to me.''

Reconnecting with Jim in her mind is like reconnecting with her sexual-creative energy.

Ben spoke about his dream:

"I had a dream about dreaming. And I've become aware that I've been walking around the last few weeks as if I'm in a dream. This is an interesting insight for me because I've been wondering what's going on. I feel that my life is becoming kind of like a dream in that what I'm doing (taking a leave of absence and going away to paint for a semester) is something that I never would have done if I had functioned in my usual obsessive-compulsive way, which is to make huge operations out of even the most minimal events. And in order to have allowed myself to do this, I had to allow myself to just let myself go, and not think about it; just do it. I feel something has propelled me into doing this that is almost unconscious—that I haven't thought carefully about it, and I haven't really planned this event. I'm not anxious about it, I'm not frantic. I've just sort of *allowed* myself to do this. And all the time I've been saying to myself, 'I wish I could let myself go and do some of the things that I've always wanted to do.' I realize now that's what I'm doing.

"For example, I do things I enjoy—like playing tennis or going to concerts. I also started getting my hundreds of travel photos together into albums; for years they've been lying in large shopping bags, unsorted. I almost have to do all this unconsciously. I'm operating differently. I'm allowing myself to be guided by the pleasure of things, the excitement. I'm much more spontaneous. Yesterday, out of the blue, I decided to go to a Mets–Giants baseball game. It was Sunday. And I managed to get a last-minute ticket.

What I've wanted to do for a long time is chuck this spinning rational head of mine and get to some other thing. And I am."

FIFTH WEEK

People's dreaming life continued to play a large role in their waking lives. This basically means that they were allowing their unconscious to filter through in ways that had not happened in the past.

BEN: "I had a dream of an abstract painting with geometric shapes. A very casual yellow rectangular shape dominates the painting. I very rarely remember any colors in a dream. And I made a painting of it."

MARK: "I had a funny experience today while I was awake. After I had been working on my book, I had an hour before going to the university. And I turned on some Chopin nocturnes. I was in a pre-sleep state. The music was beautiful. In my mind I was playing along with the music. And all of a sudden, the playing that I was pretending to do merged into my using the computer to type my book. And I suddenly had this thought: 'If only I could write the book the way I would be playing.' "

ANNE: "I had a dream which brought out how much I want to be free, but work ties me down and traps me. I'm angry because I'm stuck. In my dream, young adults are invading my space. They come into my living room, use my telephone. My home is my only refuge, and it's not peaceful because I'm concentrating on the noise they are making.'' (In working on the dream, which we did during the session, she realized that the kids were her students, and additionally, she envied them for their freedom; they were artists.) "The dream," she said, "was telling me I could relax. It's all in my head. The kids are really harmless. I just have this preoccupation that I'm being put in a situation where I'm out of control. So I feel like I always have to be on guard.''

GINNY: "I put a call into Jim finally, but I got his answering machine. That night I dreamt I was looking for someone, I don't know who, and walking through a maze of corridors. I kept wandering down hallways but always found myself alone. . . . The next afternoon, I found out from Jim's brother that Jim is away for two weeks on business.''

SIXTH WEEK

Several people reported that they had made changes in their lives without consciously trying to. Mark spoke first:

"Last week, as I mentioned, I was listening to piano music, and I had a fantasy that I was playing. And then I had the fantasy that if only I could write on my word processor the way I would play—with abandon—wouldn't that be wonderful! So I decided to sit down at my word processor and just try to do that. But I didn't do it with my book. I did it instead with some other reports that have been hanging over my head. And actually I've done ten of the twelve horrible reports that I had to do, and they've gone very fast. So now, if I can do two more by next Thursday, then I can sit down and do the book. Usually these things are so laborious, and I'm so obsessive about them."

GINNY: "I asked my dream: 'Should I call Jim again?' I had a dream something like the one last week. I was in another maze, and I walked down a long corridor this time to a room. I opened the door and there was Jim, sitting with his back to me. I whispered his name but he did not answer. I walked over to him and put my hand on his shoulder, and he began to fade away. Just his jacket remained on the back of the chair. I became frightened and woke up.

"The dream really upset me, and I kept thinking about it all day. A couple of mornings later, I began to remember how difficult it was to communicate with Jim when we were together after the first few months. He'd say loving things to me but his feelings didn't seem to be there. I often thought he wasn't listening to me or wasn't interested in what I was saying. I couldn't reach him. I broke up with him twice. It didn't work either time. I still love him but I know it will only turn out badly again. I guess all those other dreams I had earlier about Jim were wish dreams. I feel very deflated, and I'm not sure what I'm going to do."

BEN: "I risked a new style in my painting. I scraped the paint off the canvas with a palette knife. Generally I paint more realistically. This was with more freedom. I also called a friend I hadn't talked to in four-and-a-half years. Out of the blue I called him. He's living right near me. It's nice to be in touch with him again."

ANNE: "Earlier in the week I had many on-going dreams

involving trains, subways and buses, walking on platforms—searching dreams that started as long as twenty years ago up to the present time. Sometimes a period of a year or so will go by between dreams. They usually involve not being able to find the right train or being on a train or bus which turns out to go in the wrong direction. I'm lost in a strange neighborhood looking in vain at street signs which mean nothing to me. Or walking through stations while many trains go by, never the right one. Or I can't find the door to get on the train with Mayor Koch who asks me for my autograph—which I start to write but can't finish because I've forgotten my name. . . .

"My train dreams leave me with a feeling that I'm really lost and wandering in my life without direction and without purpose. When I'm feeling this way there are a lot of missed trains and wrong trains. So I think it very definitely is a reflection of my state of mind when I start having these train dreams. . . ."

(This was two steps backward from the feelings of hope and elation she had in the fourth week—which can be par for the course. As people inch forward, progress sometimes brings out more clearly the unresolved barriers to success. The group reminded her of this.)

"The good news is that I took the risk of bringing up to my chairman what bothered me, and he apologized and said he didn't want me to leave."

(Recall the dream she reported during the third week of the workshop, of a man wrestling with an ape.)

"It has now been resolved. And things have been much more pleasant. I told him when he acted like that I didn't know how to handle it, but I had the feeling that perhaps he wanted me to leave. And he said, 'Oh, no, you handled it right. I was haranguing you, so you walked out.' He apologized and that's resolved.

Later that day I got up the courage to ask him if he could rearrange my schedule next semester so I can have more classes back-to-back. (That would give me some free days for my painting.) Guess what! He said, 'Yes.' "

SEVENTH WEEK

For homework I had asked the group to focus on an image they remembered as they were drifting off to sleep. Their reactions follow:

MARK: "When I thought of my image, it was a soothing one. It was an antique vase filled with lilies of all sizes and colors. It was the best night's sleep in a long time."

BEN: "I had a similar experience."

GINNY: "I dreamt I was standing in a circle with other people, watching a street juggler perform. I realized after a minute or two that the juggler was a woman who had blond hair like me. She was juggling several pins at the same time and looked very self-confident. When I woke up, I felt terrific. I realized that was me juggling my life and staying centered."

ANNE: "I had a very interesting dream this week. There was a tree with the roots exposed; the roots were entwined around large cobblestones. I lay down on those roots and tried to get in there. I think it is such a wonderful image; I'm trying to get down to my core, to something at the root of everything."

BEN: "It's amazing. I'm starting to remember my dreams. That was one of my purposes in coming to the group. My dream is that I am with a bunch of people. I look out and there is a landscape I am fascinated with. It is not realistic. And I think, 'I want to paint this landscape.' The sun is going down, and I have to catch it immediately. And before I can get my stuff, it goes away. It disappears. And I say to myself, 'But I want to paint that landscape. . . .'

"I didn't think that I would ever paint landscapes— it's one of those things that I'm least interested in painting, except that I thought to myself, 'When you go to Italy, you won't know what to paint. Maybe you can paint landscapes. After all, they do resemble the human form.' "

Anne offered Ben a suggestion based on her years of painting: "When you have a dream like that, it's an opening to free your work. Try to capture the feeling of your image. Don't try for perfect memory. And just do it as something very loose, very free. Tear colored paper or whatever. Keep working toward the feeling of that image. You may come up with something really really good." This is an example of how group members helped one another.

EIGHTH WEEK

This was our last meeting, and the group talked about what the experience had been for them, and the changes that had taken place.

GINNY: "I started to make new connections. I'm learning how I can use my dreams and my emotions and my physical activity. I'm starting to think everything is one and the same. It's not as if that's my *career*. I can't differentiate any more between me, my playwork, my real work. It's not like that. I'm starting to integrate a lot of different aspects of my life. I think the most important thing I've learned here is how to direct my dreams, how to communicate with myself through my dreams—more consciously and unconsciously. I'm able to ask myself a question and answer it. And it's wild. I feel a lot more powerful, a lot more in control, knowing that these avenues are open and that these forms of communication do exist. I feel closer to myself and more at one with myself, and able to say, 'Okay, I want to talk about this and talk about that.' It's really great. I never considered it before, not in that way. . . . And I'm relieved about the decision I came to about Jim."

For a long time, Ginny kept hoping Jim would come and rescue her, and help her rediscover herself. In her version of Ben's dream, she felt both her female and male parts were equally strong, but the outside circumstance was the absence of Jim. Once she began to express herself on her own, she didn't need Jim in the same way. She was always dreaming of Jim "helping" her, but she, in fact, was accomplishing things on her own. Because she once changed her life under Jim's influence, she believed this was the only way, it was familiar. So she clung to the past rather than moving forward. During the workshop, she managed to realize a garden and a workspace—two of her goals— through her own efforts. By the end of the workshop, she was feeling more integrated, self-realized, and confident in her own creative powers.

ANNE: "I feel this workshop has really affected my life. One of the most interesting things is to be able to have an image in my dream, and then activate it or realize it a few days later and find the close connection. Even last night in my dream, for the first time that I was aware of it, I had a moment where I was lucid.[14] I told myself I'd have to push myself through that wall to get out. And things that seemed impossible have begun to happen in real life. I've been pushing through the psychological walls that I've had.

"Then last night in my dream, I was stretching and looking at the world upside-down, looking at people from their shoes up. So when I was jogging today in the park I told myself to look at the world that way. And it was very strange. The gravity was so obvious. I almost thought people could float up. It just made everything seem so light, and not as heavy and serious as I sometimes take life to be. And it was as if I were telling myself in the dream, 'Look at the world in a different way. Gravity is not holding you down.'

"Another thing is that I'm writing again. I had stopped writing about ten years ago. And, in terms of my art, I take individual images seriously now instead of seeing them as fantasies. I see them now as important symbols in my life, and I use them in my painting . . . I write my dream down and I sketch, and that helps me with my art. I get deeper into myself that way. I'm pushing that unconscious part of myself to be conscious, and it's not a freaky thing anymore. It's sort of a gift that we're all given.

"Actually, going into my dreams has started me thinking more about writing than drawing. I had a dream of reading many paperback books, each story more fascinating than the next. As I ripple through the

books and see the printed words, the stories are completely understood in my mind, kind of short-hand
dream-reading. I'm not actually reading the words, but
I'm looking at the pages and I say, 'Oh, that's an interesting story.' I think in my dream I can write a story
like that: about a woman completely alone in a woody
wilderness who by accident becomes trapped, pinned
to the ground, and who, with great ingenuity, effects
her release. Later that evening, I wrote that story. I feel
excited and pleased that this is another facet of my
creativity.

"On a general note, I'm striving toward integration.
But I'm still pulling in different directions. I'm still the
body that's in sections. I'll have to work on this for a
while. I do feel encouraged, however, especially about
the dream I had last week of getting down to my roots."

An additional note: Anne, who wanted to fulfill herself
more completely as an artist, had to hold down a job to
help support her family. One of her problems was time.
Another was feeling too weak to survive as a woman. A
third was to integrate all the conflicting desires in her life
so that she could focus on what was most important. She
began to feel her own strength, which helped her to assert
herself with her chairman, including asking him for a
more compact work week so that she would have additional days to paint. She began to break through psychological walls, and also began to explore writing again.

MARK: "Several things happened to me in this workshop
that were very dramatic. The incubation exercises and
then the dreams helped me understand more clearly
why I was having some of the anxieties and self-doubts
about writing and speaking. And what's happening as

a result is that I'm really enjoying my writing. I look forward to getting involved and doing it, and I'm resenting distractions. I've also had some invitations to speak that have excited me rather than left me feeling burdened by them. So I'm feeling much lighter.

"I put some things together about what was holding me back, what some of the self-doubts and anxieties were about. I think the dreams were startling. Several things became very clear that couldn't escape my attention. And the most important thing was that image I had when I was listening to music. And I had the feeling of how nice it would be to sit down and write the way one played the piano. And that brought together the lack of encouragement, actually discouragement, I'd had as a child, for anything either intellectual or musical, and what a struggle it's been for me to achieve—but I have. Yet my achievements have always been in the absence of any familial recognition. So I've been trying to play the piano when I'm writing. . . . I'm discovering too that my writing is becoming less academic—which I had been struggling for. It's coming more from my feelings now, my intuition, my whole self. The music is helping me to connect to that part of me.

"At the beginning of the workshop I was aware of the absence of someone to spur me on, to share the creative process with, as my wife had done. I realized that in order to get this need filled, I needed to talk more and share my ideas about the creative process. I couldn't do this in an isolated way. I stopped holding back when I was with people and began talking about what I was writing about, thinking about, and some of the struggles I was having. That revitalized me. When I sat down to write, I wasn't so lonely."

Mark's commentary sums up the changes that took place for him. The workshop helped him work through some of the survival anxieties and guilts he had concerning his wife's death and his unresolved childhood conflicts, in order to reach the state of freedom and enjoyment he eventually achieved. In addition, he invented a technique of writing that at least one other person in the workshop adopted with success. Listening to music while writing (composing) on a computer enabled the other group member to get into the rhythmic-emotional, moving part of herself. Her writing improved and was a more pleasurable experience.

BEN: "Yesterday I had a surge of confidence. I knew exactly what I wanted to do. A clarity that I've been looking for for months. As you know, I've had this idea of painting the human form in a new way, in a way it had not been painted before. I've had this idea all along in a vague sense. And yesterday I was working on this little painting; and I read an article that verbalized the ideas I had not been quite able to verbalize. And I suddenly felt very confident about what I wanted to do. I really felt I wanted to do it. So when I go away, I know what I want to paint.

"In general, I have become much more aware of my unconscious, many times to a great degree. I was always afraid of it. I don't feel so fearful now. For a long time I was constantly thinking about how I could express myself. It feels like everything is percolating. The workshop made my whole life feel more full. I think there's something inside me now, and that I have a lot to say."

Ben had begun to realize his goal of unblocking himself as a painter. He is also trusting his unconscious a great deal more and feels his life is fuller.

HOW TO FORM YOUR OWN GROUP

If you wish to form your own creativity–dream group, first and foremost look for people who are dedicated to tapping their creativity. You may want to focus your group around a special theme, such as problem solving, relationships, healing, or dreams. You can start by posting a notice in a church or school, or running an ad in a local newspaper. But do weed out the dilettantes from the serious. When the group meets, you will need to set up simple but strict guidelines:

1. Have respect for each person's contribution and allow time to share his or her ideas, results, and process—but within time limits so that no individual dominates the group. You may want to use a stopwatch, setting it at five minutes per person.

2. Listen without interpreting the content of someone else's material.

3. Maintain confidentiality, which means that what is discussed in the group stays within the group. This provides safety for people to be honest about their lives and feelings, permits trust to develop, and keeps the intensity of the group interaction intact.

These guidelines are essential for continuing the group and gaining the maximum experience from it.

PART FOUR

Verification

11

LIVING
YOUR CREATIVITY

Y ou've now reached the most challenging and rewarding step of your journey. You've had creative hunches and insights. And this is the time to make them come true in your life. There is no better way to enlarge and enrich your life than to take risks. It is one thing to see the solution, to have the vision; it is another to actualize it and make it a part of everyday living. If you are still wondering why it is so important to tap your unconscious, just remember that when you are in the process of bringing forth buried memories, dreams, and other imagery from your unconscious, you are filled with energy, you feel excited and alive, and you don't know where your unconscious will lead you. If you work in the creative arts, the sense of life is conveyed to your audience. A polished, slick work may do nothing to an audience because once something is known, no matter how interesting, it is in a sense already dead. That is why the element of risk is necessary. It brings to life the roots of your creativity. And that is why the actress Shami Chaiken deliberately leaves something unprepared when she is performing, so that she can experience a risk and bring a new unknown element to her performance. Many people who have participated in the creativity workshop have changed their lives through the risks they have taken; you will see how shortly.

The first question to ask yourself is: Am I willing to follow my dream? And by "dream" here, I am referring to your aspirations, your wishes. If so, you must take risks. All risks demand a certain degree of courage. Not all are big risks, but some are. Consider those individuals who have risked their reputations and even their lives to follow their dreams. Mahatma Gandhi, India's great leader, fasted while he was in jail and even risked starvation to follow his spiritual goal. Fasting was a nonviolent action to win India's freedom from British rule; and he succeeded.

Thomas Eakins, the great American artist, defied convention to follow his beliefs, and because of it he never enjoyed fame during his lifetime. Art, he believed, must show the truth, not what others would like it to be. During the time Eakins was an instructor at the Pennsylvania Academy of Fine Art, students worked only from plastic copies of classic sculpture. Eakins decided to use live models. In the midst of one of his classes, Eakins removed the loincloth from a live male model to demonstrate that the pelvis was central to the movement and balance of the human figure. This action shocked the art world, and he was asked to resign. He continued to paint, however, despite mounting hardship and struggle. His greatness was recognized only years after his death.

Fortunately, not all who dare to follow their dream,

especially when it conflicts with accepted belief, suffer the same unhappy fate as did Eakins. Sometimes a person risks a reputation already earned. One such risk-taker was Hollywood actor, director, and scriptwriter Woody Allen. Allen turned his back on comedy, the avenue that had earned him fame and success, to express a philosophical and serious side of himself, a side that his audiences never fathomed. Movies such as *Interiors* and *The Other Woman* are somber, stark studies of modern life. His audience wondered, could this be the same person who wrote *Annie Hall* or *Everything You Always Wanted to Know About Sex*? Allen took the chance of being panned by the critics and spurned by his audience to risk a different approach to his work.

Another risk-taker is fashion photographer Richard Avedon. Avedon's work, *In the American West*, went against everything he had done in the past. The photographs were cruel, dissecting studies of drifters, waitresses, people from mental hospitals. Avedon, famous for his photographs of fashion models and celebrities, exposed himself to the possibility of devastating criticism when he published these photographs. His willingness to take risks, however, is the very quality that had earned him his reputation in the first place. He is one of the first photographers to make a fashion model look like a real moving human being rather than a mannikin.

Susan B. Anthony was a woman who struggled all her adult years to achieve a goal that, sadly, she was never to realize during her lifetime. In her active campaigning for women's rights, she was constantly at war with society. She published a periodical on women's rights called *Revolution*. The publication folded, but Susan B. Anthony became known throughout the nation. And it was her efforts that led to the vote for women fourteen years after her death.

I would venture to say that every human being that has ever made a contribution to society was a risk-taker. Some boldly followed their convictions despite opposition. Others took risks even when they felt they were on shakey ground.

According to the renowned 20th-century writer Anaïs Nin, we must know what our wishes are, for without this knowledge, "we have no strength, we have no inspirational visions."[15] Nin often took dreams as her guide. In one auspicious dream she climbed into an old abandoned boat she'd seen in the yard of some friends, and she traveled for twenty years, making an incredible journey. Soon after this dream she saw an ad in the newspaper that said "Houseboat For Rent." She rented the boat for two years, at only ten dollars a month, and made her dream come true. Thus she carried out her inner journey in her waking life as the dream foretold.

Following in Nin's footsteps, a woman in a creativity workshop took a risk that was also based on a dream. She dreamt she was in jail and someone was coming to let her out. In her dream, she was also the person letting herself out of the jail. But instead of freeing herself, she merely changed the terms of imprisonment. When she awoke, she reflected upon the dream and realized: "That's the kind of person I am. Once I make a decision, it obviously forecloses all other options. I end up losing freedom regardless of what I do." She asked herself what kind of freedom she wanted in life and one of her wishes was to be looser, less shy with people. She was always waiting for others to tell her what they wanted, and then she would respond. So she took the risk of being herself, saying more of what *she* felt. She risked this in four different situations. "The result," she said, "was that I felt comfortable, the other people felt comfortable, and I felt closer to everyone."

Taking a risk is the best way to get yourself out of a rut, and it has wonderful side effects such as broadening your outlook and making you feel absolutely terrific about yourself. Sometimes it is simply a question of doing something entirely different from what you've done before. It could be as simple as going to the drugstore and buying bubble bath. It could be trying flower arranging, making a mask, or adopting a pet. Once you move from your habitual stance, you change your energy and expose yourself to a different set of circumstances. Life begins to feel exciting again, and so much more is possible.

My first serious introduction to the world of risk-taking occurred when I was in my early twenties. Sometimes when I get stuck now, I remind myself of this experience. At that time, I was going through a phase where my life felt predictable and boring. I complained to someone I hardly knew about this, and this someone, a wise person, said, "Take a risk." I waited to hear more, but that was all he offered. It was up to me to decide what risk to take. So I began making up risks and taking them right on the spot. For example, while waiting in line at the motor vehicles department, I took the risk of talking to three strangers, chosen out of sheer proximity: two to the front of me, one to the rear. I am not one to talk to strangers. The experience made the time fly by and was memorable because it cut the tedium. One person was quite interesting. Waiting in line changed from an irritating experience to a pleasant one.

But the risk that was a major influence in my life was truly mundane. I was having breakfast at the counter of a coffee shop, and I was hungry that morning. I ordered orange juice, corned beef hash with an egg, toast, and coffee. The waitress listened to my order, then shouted to the cook: "One Clean-Up-the-Kitchen"—slang for corned beef hash. I ate it anyway. My appetite was ravenous that day, and I still longed for one more piece of toast. "I can't ask for that," I told myself. "The waitress will think I'm a pig. It's just not done. No one orders three pieces of toast." Then my line of thinking went to "Ah, this can be my next risk. The worst scenario is that I could be mortified. But they wouldn't dare arrest me or throw me out." My heart beat rapidly as I asked softly (so that only the waitress could hear me) for another piece of toast. "What?" she snapped. I steeled myself. And calmly and assertively and with full voice, I said: "May I have a third piece of toast?" No one paid any attention to me, except the waitress who said cheerfully, "Surely." The relief and gratitude I felt grew into a major insight for me. I realized how much I had been trapped by conventions and rules, how restricted and afraid I was to do anything out of the ordinary. Then I began to contemplate the absurdity of many of our customs. For example, why not eat spaghetti and meatballs for breakfast instead of ham and eggs! I'm sure some people do. Why eat soup with a spoon rather than just raising the bowl to your lips and slurping? When you are a weekend guest in someone's house, why neatly fold sheets that will only be disarranged in the washing machine anyway? If someone else dreamt up these arbitrary customs, why can't I make up my own? Why do I have to follow theirs? All these customs, of course, originated with someone doing them first and others agreeing to them, so that they became acceptable forms of behavior. But when the rules become more important than one's comforts or needs, they are stultifying. I thought about the absurdity of the rigidities and discomforts we put ourselves through to do the right thing. And then I told myself to stop using the editorial "we."

I reflected on how the true thinkers and doers of society live more by their own rules than those of others. And for some reason I thought of Vincent van Gogh—a true visionary and nonconformist. What freedom is gained from making your own rules instead of following someone else's! Since I do believe I have good enough sense and judgment, I decided to try to live by my own rules rather than those arbitrary rules that often have little to do with me. It is difficult to live a creative life when your greater concern is "Am I doing what *they* want, am I pleasing others?"

I tell this story in detail to illustrate how even the tiniest of risks can lead to the greatest of results. So remember, your risks need not be earth-shaking. Let them make sense to you within the context of your own life, and do use your judgment about them. Don't take risks that could place you behind bars or that could endanger your own life or the lives of others. That said, we're ready for the next exercise.

Exercise 27:
TAKING RISKS

Think of what it is you truly want in your life. Is it having a deeper involvement in your work? Changing careers? Finding a lover? Expressing more of yourself to others? Learning a new skill? Whatever it is, ask yourself how you can actualize it. When you take a risk, you may be going against a habitual pattern. And you may feel dread rather than excitement and pleasure. Focus on the new spaces and new opportunities this risk may open up for you, and do it anyway. It's perfectly fine to start small—such as ordering three pieces of toast.

Take three risks every day for a week. Not only will this

get you into the habit of risk-taking, but it will challenge your imagination in the creating of new risks. It will also bring you smack up against what it is you want in your life and what it is that holds you back.

After you've taken these risks, write them in your journal, giving a full account of what you did and what results you got. Also make note of what you learned by doing them.

A free-lance consultant never charged the fees that could make his work a pleasure rather than the drudgery it had become. He was under so much pressure to make enough money just to survive that he could no longer enjoy the work he had chosen to do and actually had sacrificed a high-paying job for. His tendency to undermine his own performance, even though others applauded it, came from a childhood lacking in parental support. He grew up believing he was not as gifted as he really was. Realizing that his low fees were a result of his poor self-image, he took a risk: he decided to ask double what he normally would ask. His client never batted an eyelash; he got the job and walked away with the idea he would ask triple the next time around. As he continued to risk asking higher fees, he fell back in love with his work again. And he continued to enjoy it just as long as he asked for the fees he deserved.

A woman who had been taught since early childhood that her purpose in life was to serve others took the risk of going against her pattern. It was painfully hard for her to ask anyone for anything. She even found it difficult to tell a man, who had invited her, that she wanted to go up in his small plane. But she made herself do this and he was delighted. Once up in the air and having circled around awhile, he said to her, "Now you take the wheel." She had never flown a plane before in her life and was shaking like a leaf when she took hold of the wheel. She kept seeing herself in a computer game flying a plane and overturning it. The man, however, assured her that she couldn't overturn the plane. She flew the plane for several minutes before he took the wheel again, and she was terrified the whole time. However, flying stimulated her sense of adventure. It was something important in a life she regarded as very neat and predictable. And so, to add adventure to her life, she took the risk of signing up for flying lessons. This would be the one activity in her life that could give her the sense of freedom she craved.

A teacher didn't like the way her class's textbooks were written, so she decided to write her own class plans instead, based on what was actually occurring in each previous class. As a result, the classes became more focused and meaningful to the students, and she was pleased that she had replaced a tired formula with her own live inventiveness.

She took a second risk in order to overcome her fear of intimacy. She agreed to visit a new acquaintance who lived in the suburbs of Philadelphia. This is her account of what took place:

> "What usually happens to me is that after a day or half-a-day, I get scared about the closeness with the person, and I start getting sleepy and they get a little bored, and I'm ready to go home. But I stuck with it, and I said my feelings out loud. Like, 'I'm feeling a little tired. I usually feel tired when I'm getting a little itchy about spending that much time with someone.' That's all I said. Then I added, 'I think maybe a cup of coffee will work.' And I had a cup of coffee and that seemed to work. . . .
>
> "Then I decided to stay even a little longer than I expected. The risks I took concerning my friend

had to do with my thinking she wouldn't want to do what I wanted to do. So I asked it in a way that it was a question. I said I would like to go into the city. There were a couple of things I wanted to pick up there. I said it in such a way that it was up to her to say yes or no, and either would have been O.K. with me. I left myself open a little more. And we did everything. I didn't find the antique clock I was looking for, so instead of getting frustrated and a little angry, I said to her, 'Why don't we have a cappuccino in that little Italian expresso cafe over there.' We went into a very lovely restaurant. And I stayed longer than I expected to and came home on the Metroliner, spending a lot more money than I would normally spend. This all came from a desire on my part to loosen up and be more creative, more flexible, and more brilliant.''

For many of us, one of the scariest risks is to express ourselves fully and allow others to see it. As children, many of us were ridiculed or rejected by insensitive parents, relatives, teachers, or others when we attempted to express ourselves. And we learned that it was easier to hold back or even repress our feelings. When you take a risk, you may once again experience the *fear* of being hurt as you were as a child. And that is a big risk. I hope that you have learned, through these pages and elsewhere, that it's the ignorance, fear, and envy of others that inhibit your self-expression, and that when you express yourself honestly, you are loving yourself and giving to others as well. As an adult, you no longer need the approval that children so desperately need for both their survival and development—even though you may feel you do.

Over the years I have delighted in observing the risks

that people have taken in the creativity workshops and classes. It is gratifying to see them step up to a new plateau where life offers so many more possibilities. As people become more aware of their potential, they long to express it. This is where risk enters the picture.

Molly, for example, suffered from paralyzing stage fright. She had a beautiful singing voice and her greatest wish was to sing in a Broadway show. But her fear got in the way of any satisfaction. She blamed herself and bitterly acknowledged that fear stopped her from doing what she knew she could do so well. Finally in the last meeting of a creativity workshop, she took a risk; she said she would sing, but asked us not to comment either yea or nea. Her first efforts ended in her blushing and backing off. Eventually, using all her will it seemed, she forced out one line of a song. And that was all it took. A few months later, I received an invitation to an off-Broadway production of a hit musical in which she had a minor role. She was thrilled that she had finally broken through her fear and could get credit from the outside world for her talent.

A man terrified of his own anger, and everyone else's too, took the risk of expressing some of his anger toward two members of the workshop. This was, in his words, "something I never under any circumstances would do. It helped me a lot, and I'm now more in touch with myself in a lot of ways."

A retired playwright finally risked doing the thing he had always wanted to do but had found excuses not to. He called three studios and made appointments to make television commercials.

A woman started to write an article she had been only *thinking* about doing; she took the second risk of writing a song, and the third risk of telling her boyfriend about it. Her fourth risk was to sing it to him.

Taking some risks can almost be like facing a phobia. You may be trembling with fear, but once you have confronted the dreaded task it becomes a little easier next time. And each time you do it, it becomes easier and easier.

Taking risks is a never-failing way to develop self-confidence, even if you don't start off that way. And this new feeling of self-worth is a stepping stone to taking more risks. Sue Rene Bernstein, a cabaret singer, claims: "Having a strong point of view helps in taking risks. I know who I want to present up there. Therefore I'm not afraid to put forth a piece of material that's a bit challenging. This is who I am. If you feel your own sense of what you want to say strongly enough, that in itself allows for a certain cushion and allows you to take risks in your material. To take these risks you have to rid yourself of any judgment. For me, it all comes down to one thing: to be able to take risks as a performer and put forth my dark side and use my emotions all involve creating safety. Our creativity comes from finding what is most unique within us and then relating it in a way that makes it universal."

Georgia O'Keeffe believed in herself when, at the age of thirty, she destroyed all her previous work because it had been influenced by other artists. Instead of depending on others, she painted only what was in her head.

Amelia Earhart overcame her fears when she flew solo across the Atlantic Ocean in 1932. As one of the first to do this, she must certainly have suffered moments of fear and trepidation.

And both Maria Callas, the great opera singer and Helen Hayes, the great actress, had to be pushed on stage to perform. As I have emphasized again and again, through one's creativity one can safely express things one otherwise might not be able to in life. An actor confessed that he could reveal the most intimate aspects of himself in front of hundreds of people but had to hide them from the "significant others" in his life. It is no secret that many actors and actresses are often very shy people.

A very shy woman in one of my workshops reported:

> "Somebody I work with started coming up in my dreams. In my dreams he is just always a really good guy. He can be there for you. I had a dream that I am walking in the light with him. And we are just talking. This is somebody who I don't have romantic feelings toward, but with whom I always feel a little shy and distant. I decided to take the risk and tell him about a problem I was having. But I realized that wasn't the real risk. The real risk was saying to him, 'You're really wonderful and caring, and that means a lot to me.' So I did, and he just kind of blushed and bumbled. There was a really good feeling. It was wonderful. I'm taking the risk now of living my dreams."

Risks frequently come out of hardship. It takes great courage to suffer a blow and then get back on your feet again. Frances Lear was in her sixties when she and her famous husband, Norman, divorced. Of course, it helped that she received $112 million in the divorce settlement. Nonetheless, with no magazine experience whatsoever, Frances Lear used $30 million to start a brand-new genre of magazine, called *Lear's*—for the woman over forty. This was to be a magazine for a woman at the peak of her power and allure. "I wanted to focus attention on this woman as something other than what she was perceived to be. She was not this menopausal, depressed, empty-nested person whose life was finished."[16]

Others less sophisticated and well connected than

Frances Lear also take risks that are inventive and cou-
rageous: the teen-age secretary, for example, who wanted
to be an actress and opened up her own acting school.
First, she found a large loft in the city at a time when
space was still cheap. She worked fifteen hours a day to
support her acting school, which she started in the loft.
She ran the school successfully for six months, and hired
some of the best acting teachers in New York to work for
her. She never admitted she was the director, because she
feared no one would listen to a seventeen-year-old. She
said instead that she was the director's assistant and under
that guise did all the hiring, firing, and admissions.

A woman songwriter risked sending one of her songs
by certified mail to the copyright office in Washington,
D.C., and the same night risked performing it. She had
called a café that presented amateur night once a month.
She sang the song she had written and reported that people had applauded and some had even stood up and
shouted "Bravo."

When people follow their wishes, as we have already
witnessed, they must often put themselves on the line. Mus-
sorgsky, for example, started off as an officer in the Russian
army. Because of his love of music he resigned his commission at age eighteen, and threw himself into composing.

An engineer who had wanted to write fiction but could
never make the leap, took an event from someone else's
dream during a workshop and wrote a story based on it.
"The little bit of time I spent on it," he reported, "showed
me, in fact, that yes, I could literally make up a story built
around just one little element. I've done a lot of stream-
of-consciousness writing, but for whatever reason, oddly
enough, I was having trouble making something up. In fact,
there was even this moment in my mind of thinking, 'But
this isn't true. There is some sort of falseness about it.' But
I just kinda pushed through that feeling long enough to

keep going with it, and I began to think, 'Well, okay, that's what people do. I mean it's not like a new idea. . . .' "

What may seem like a risk to one person may not be at all risky to another. A busy executive had no time for a haircut. Rather than continue through life with a shaggy head, he took the risk of cutting his own hair. "Not as good as the barber," he commented, "but it will do in a pinch." This kind of risk fits into the category of doing things we ordinarily depend on others to do, such as hanging a picture, putting up bookshelves, pumping our own gas. Minor as they may seem, when we do them ourselves, we undo our feelings of helplessness and increase our sense of accomplishment and self-esteem. And we build up our courage to take on more formidable risks.

The feeling of success leads to a wish for more success. It's a great motivator. On the other hand, some people may be spurred on by feelings of failure. To compensate for these awful feelings, some people try even harder to go after what they want. One woman was tired of seeming like a drudge to others. People always regarded her as serious and deadly dull. And whenever she attempted to say something humorous, people took it the wrong way and didn't realize it was meant to be funny. She wanted to show people she had a light side and a sense of humor, so she took the risk of performing at a church event. The idea had occurred to her one day while she was sitting in a subway train. Her eyes were closed, and an image of a mime moving jerkily to classical music crossed her field of vision. She found this extraordinarily funny. The mime was jerking around to Beethoven's Fifth Symphony. She decided to dress up, not as a mime but as a chicken, and boogey to Beethoven's Fifth Symphony herself. She created her costume out of things she already owned; yellow tights, her husband's sweatshirt, a woolen winter hat into which she stuffed all of her hair, and a feather duster that looked perfect as a tail. She then bought whiteface makeup. When her moment arrived that Friday night, she asked the monitor to put her record of Beethoven's Fifth Symphony on the phonograph. She faced her audience dressed as a chicken, her heart pounding. She boogied and "buck bucked," and they howled. A man she had known for years came over to her later and said, "I can't believe you did that; it was wonderful."

One of the most important effects of risk-taking is its power to heal. Not only are you taking chances that can solve problems, you also are widening your boundaries, enlarging your possibilities. You are no longer waiting for others to give you what you want and need or for situations to arise that will make your dreams come true. The characters in *Waiting for Godot* by Samuel Beckett stayed in exactly the same place all their lives and never lived at all. Through both creativity and risk-taking, you *actively* give yourself what you need. Perhaps you wanted acknowledgement from others and never got it; now you can give it to yourself. Freud, speaking on a grand scale, was right on target when he said that the artist gains from expressing his fantasy what he had only hoped to achieve through his fantasy: wealth, glory, fame, and love.

Freud knew whereof he spoke. Although not a creative artist, he himself was an amazing risk-taker. He challenged established ideas in a variety of areas, particularly in the most dangerous, the area of sexuality. He outraged his contemporaries by insisting that children have sexual feelings. And he also disagreed with the medical profession, which maintained that dreams were only hallucinations; Freud insisted they were the "royal road to the unconscious" and loaded with meaning. He persisted in his ideas despite the hostile opposition they engendered. And as a result, the world has greatly profited.

So reward yourself by taking a risk. And then take another.

12

CONCLUSION: HERE'S LOOKING AT YOU

It's time to take an inventory. Has something opened up, have you had flashes of insight? Are you more in touch with your interests, your vitality? Are you listening to your fantasies and wishes and expressing them creatively—"following your bliss," as Joseph Campbell has advised? It's so important to tap the energy that enables you to do whatever you wish to do. By enjoying your creative self, you can feel as the painter did who said, "My painting tells me what I care about in the world" or the writer who confided, "My work *is* what I want to think about." Knowing what you want in your life allows you to follow your aspirations, can even make you obsessive about what you are doing, and makes you care more about the world you live in. Creativity is not about the appearances of things, it's about the inner life. "Art is not handicraft," Tolstoy wrote. "It is the transmission of feelings the artist has experienced."

Your dreams are a primary source of your creativity. By using the wonderful powers of your conscious mind— your perceptions, your cognitive thought—you can tap the creativity hidden in your dreams. You can also draw upon other creative resources during your waking state, such as your five senses, your fantasies, your ability to play, your humor, and your childhood memories.

The exercises in this book are meant to call forth your creativity, during both your waking and sleeping states. The quality of your conscious life affects the intensity of your dreams, and so they complement one another. Research has shown that rapid eye movement (REM) dreaming is heightened when you learn a new skill.[17] By stimulating the conscious mind, dreaming is intensified; and this intensified dreaming, in turn, fuels your creativity during the waking state.

You must also look at what interferes with your creativity, such as the negative messages you learned in childhood, your need for perfection, comparing yourself with others, your wish to please, and your fears of failure *and* success. These blocks, unless addressed, can handicap you for the rest of your life.

What's more, unless you actively use the insights you acquire from the exercises, they will lie dormant, will merely be nice thoughts and reveries to reflect upon. Sometimes the actions you take, based upon your insights, will evolve naturally without any effort on your part. At other times they will require risk-taking. I know full well as a therapist that all the insights in the world do not change a person unless he or she applies these insights to life. That is why I've followed Aristotle's brilliant four-step method to creativity in this book: first the *preparation* stage, then *incubation*, next *illumination*, and finally *verification*.

Note particularly the *verification* stage for the moment. Would the world ever have known the sewing machine if Elias Howe had not implemented the discovery he had made in a nightmare? (In his dream, savages were pointing their spears at him, threatening to kill him if he did not complete his sewing machine invention. In great terror he noticed eye-shaped holes near the points of their spears, and he realized *that* was where to place the holes in the machine's needles. This was the information he needed to complete his invention.) If Elias Howe had not carried out his invention, someone else might have, and Howe would never have experienced the joy and fulfillment of his contribution. "Doing" opens up new possibilities that even a dream may not provide. You see the world opening up in a new way and offering you the hope for new experience. Even a tiny glimpse of something different can be the beginning of something exciting. Verification in waking reality further feeds your dreams. It's an endless process of give and take.

Although I have separated the creative process into four distinct stages, sometimes all four stages may occur simultaneously. The method, outlined above, can bring about what philosopher and mathematician Bertrand Russell discovered only after years of trying to realize his creative goals through will. Once he let go of will, and waited patiently for his unconscious to provide the flash of insight required, he could accomplish his goals. But you need not wait.

Now, are you ready to evaluate your progress?

Exercise 28:
LOOKING BACK, LOOKING FORWARD

Look back to the first exercise you did in this book: "Where would you like to be six months from now?" Read over what you wrote, and now write in your journal about how far you've come in realizing your goals. Here are some comments from people who participated in my last creativity class and did this exercise not six months, but *two* months later:

A: I wrote that six months from now I would like to be a lot more creative person than I am today. For too long I have let traditions, social mores and customs dictate their terms to me, and, as a result, I have allowed the creative person in me to deteriorate almost to the point of extinction. Since I started this class, I have reversed the process and let fresh ideas, fresh thinking and the winds of change color my mind. And I've allowed myself the freedom of expression that I was yearning for.

B: I wrote that I wanted to be in London creating artwork with a group of artist friends. Well, I'm leaving for Europe in two months. My artwork is coming together. I draw in my sketchbook every day. I've been painting much more. I'm more focused, which was a problem for me. I've got a much clearer view of where I'm going. Everything I wrote that I wanted to be happening in six months revolved around Europe.

The exercises in this class helped me to get in

touch with myself more deeply than I could before. I will continue to keep a journal from now
on and repeat the exercises we have done.

C: Yes, I am closer to where I dreamed of being
when I wrote in our first class that I wanted to
be playing a beautiful piano. . . . About a month
ago, I decided that the job I was doing in publishing was not right for me. It was using up all
my energy and zapping my strength. I hated the
office work all the more because I wasn't doing
anything with my musical talents. I hardly sang
anymore—no more choir, no more singing at
weddings, no singing in the streets, or to my
husband for the fun of it, and no songwriting. I
was blocked, stuck, stultified. That was then.
Now I'm embarked on an exciting and terrifying
voyage. I quit my job and am taking a few weeks
to regroup and reorient and to write and get in
touch with my feelings, so I can better determine
what direction to try with my music. I am very
happy to say I worked on one of my songs today.
I'm writing again and I'm loving it. It's hard because of my *internal critics*, but you have given
me some tools to deal with them. It's not easy,
but I'm happier to be struggling and expressing
myself.

D: I still am feeling somewhat frustrated with
time issues. But, overall, things are definitely happening. Certain blocks are evaporating and I am
feeling a new clarity of purpose. I'm grateful for
my imagination, my desires, and my passions. I
suppose that the bottom line is that my relationship to myself and all other relationships in my
life (including to my creative work) are simul-

taneously expanding and becoming *simplified*. For example, I experienced wonderful feelings of bonding and unity with two of my best friends, which seem to be spilling over into so many other areas of my life. My goals remain abstract, thus it is difficult to register or recognize progress. But what I do recognize very clearly is a sense of slow, steady forward motion like being on an overnight train.

E: I am closer today to where I would ultimately like to be, because I am more at peace with myself. While I am not in the quiet, serene environment I imagine as ideal, nor am I in my ideal relationship—both of which I feel would be a stimulus to my creativity—I am in a state of mind that realizes these are mere outside factors which would only reflect inside.

I have learned to release my creative energies in new ways. Whereas before I thought I *had* to dance or write as my only creative outlets, today I use both my work and relationships as alternative releases. Just thinking about the creative process every day makes me a more content person. Waking up, remembering dreams, acting on them, and thinking in this new way is stimulating.

F: The things I wrote down two months ago as sort of a 'fantasy fling' seem less fantastic as such and much more realistic—within reach of being done. I wanted to be in a villa in Italy finishing a painting, visiting friends. And on my return home I wanted to illustrate a children's book. I am possibly closer to all of this because of my breakthrough in my art class. I've discovered a great feeling for drawing. So my fantasies are less absurd and more do-able. And I'm not afraid of them nor will I laugh at them now.

The dynamics of this workshop—which I do not fully understand intellectually—seem to have had a direct effect on my art class performance. I had been taking watercolor classes for at least three years, on and off. I really didn't have a full feeling about it, but I was sort of toying with it without getting skilled. In fact, the paintings were so poor I wouldn't show them. Actually none of them were ever completed.

But something has happened and I'm not sure I wish to examine it too closely. I find that not only do I complete paintings, but I am an extraordinarily good colorist. I am taking drawing classes too and have been astounded at how great a feeling I get from this—and also that I'm pretty good in drawing. And *I'm* the one who says that my work is good. And I don't doubt it. Some barrier has been lessened, for which I am grateful.

G: I am not really further along in any *tangible* way toward where I said I wanted to be six months from now, but perhaps I am in some intangible ways. The greatest change has been in an openness to the *possibility* of achieving my goal of becoming a more serious, disciplined writer and living part of the time away from New York City in a rural setting.

The biggest change has been the awareness of the harm my self-doubts do to my ability to act on or trust my unconscious—and the awareness that I can learn or develop the habit over time of tapping into the unconscious instead of the more superficial doubts. My confidence is growing—has actually changed over the last few weeks. The opinion that I am "not a writer" that I have carried with me from childhood, is evaporating. Instead I see that I *am* a writer and, in fact, always have been except that monumental self-doubts resulted in my closing that door, as if on something unavailable to me.

H: I joined this class in order to feel more comfortable dealing with my nightmare dream imagery, so that I might use it in my art. My goal was to use these images fluently, rather than be afraid of them. What I didn't expect, but found very useful, is the whole idea of meditation to elicit or to focus on these images. This presents to me a novel way of working in my studio— letting images appear rather than choosing them from nature.

I designed a format to deal with my "dark side" of mixing gardens on the outside (my regular subject matter) and dreams in one painting. The myth—fairy tale method of remembering the first time in childhood I felt a certain terror gave me the idea for one of my pieces. The piece, called "long-ing," shows an ocean in the distance spilling over sand dunes and into a glass vase in the foreground—sort of Magrittesque. Other rather gory things are going on also.

Using the meditation device allows me to ponder the next piece as I walk around and go about my regular job, until it's all worked out and I can sit down and paint it in one sitting. I find this extremely satisfying.

I: My six-month goals were to be accepted in a top level gallery—and to be healthy enough to enjoy it; to believe in myself; to be the *best* sculptor that I *can* be; and to resolve all the artistic problems I encounter. In addition, to deeply understand the creative drive that has made me a workaholic in art; to gracefully accept the painful moments of my work—that cause doubts in my ability; and to *realize* that I am entitled to the joy of creating my work.

I am closer to my goals. I've sold my work to selective clients. I trust myself more than before. I remain wanting to be better than I am—wondering, and even testing my creativity—and work every hour that I am able to. I enjoy the hours in my studio—and the simple things in life that inspire new forms and ideas. I like the challenge that greets me each day.

J: Where am I now? I feel that I've begun a process of awareness, of defining my authentic self. I am still "stuck" in ways my unconscious has yet to surrender. My sensitive nature is a gift I can develop, but it's been buried by emotional conflicts of the past, especially childhood, that I've yet to work through. Taking this class has moved me in the direction of exploring and desiring to become more receptive to my inner voice. I *know* I have something to express to the world. I just have to allow it to happen, let it flow freely past the barriers that have confined it over the years.

K: The amazing thing is that I discovered I was very creative all my life. But I didn't realize it. I did things I didn't look at as creativity. I would write songs or plays all evening and make dresses, and draw. And now I remind myself that my life is very creative, because I keep on doing things all the time—solving problems in new situations.

Also I thought I had no memories from my childhood. And suddenly I could recall memories from both my childhood and my teens much more easily than before. I think I'm much closer to myself as a child than before.

I needed the legitimization for my creativity that I got from your class: that I can do it, I'm allowed to do it; and I'm entitled to do it. . . . All the ideas I had and whatever I wanted to do could be realized much faster after the course. I would just sit down and say, 'Okay, now I'm doing this or that,' whereas before I just wrote down my ideas. After the course I started to *do*.

L: I'm clearly more confident in my creativity. I assume I am creative and just need opportunities to express it. I have signed up for a course to learn to draw. I have had many ideas for pieces to write. Even at work I trust myself more than I did before. I believe I know what I'm doing and I'm doing it well, even when it's not what others would do. I work for an organization that's very bureaucratic in some ways, and I am more comfortable than ever trusting that whatever I do is true—making waves, making creative decisions, and urging us all down the paths.

M: I'm now on the brink of becoming a writer, which was long overdue. I've gotten new and original ideas that were inconceivable to even think about. Also there is better communication in the family. The telephone and doorbell are ringing more with my kids, who are now grown up. I share a lot of different things with them. There is more to talk about. I didn't know how vital it was to write again. I didn't know I was about to erase the rest of my life by doing meaningless things. I didn't know what it was I wanted to do. I was unaware of the self-destruction and ill feelings that could result from not expressing myself. I have a lot of anxiety because I'm changing now . . . I enjoy myself in my work and feel guilty, I enjoy myself so much.

N: I feel I'm climbing a mountain and I'm more than half-way up—achieving all that I want to achieve. I've grown with my research job and I've grown with my art work. I'm freer and less afraid to express myself. My confidence has elevated, which has helped me to feel freer. I noticed these changes after seven weeks, but I can't pinpoint what caused them.

Look back at what *you* wrote in your first exercise, and reflect on whether any of your goals have been met. Now do the exercise *again*: "Where would you like to be six months from now?" This will help you to maintain yourself in a creative state of mind so that life continues to unfold its riches and wonders.

If you found that your progress occurred all at once in a flash of insight, that's wonderful. But, more than likely, your progress evolved through a series of realizations that occurred over time. It's like doing aerobic exercise: you may note immediate gains but the long-lasting effects do not appear until later. In the same way, real awareness is not usually instant upheaval. It can be gradual, evolutionary. Awareness puts you in power to make decisions to affect your life. That's what creativity is about. It's about having the confidence to be vulnerable to living in the open. Living in the absolute shuts off channels of energy. You limit yourself to what's safe, what's known, what's predictable or what you think is predictable. With self-awareness your life keeps changing. And as you keep tapping your awareness, you open up channels that are sometimes forbidden in society, but from which creativity flourishes.

One more thing to remember. Creativity does not necessarily go hand-in-hand with a high I.Q. A mentally retarded man, named John, once stopped me in a coffee shop. He told me he liked my earrings. And he put out his hand and introduced himself. I took his hand and in that instant felt a sense of joy. It touched something very deep in me. And I felt I was awakened from a kind of lethargy, which many of us experience as "everyday life." John had reached out and created a moment of love. I reflected on this experience later and thought, had John not been in the habit of reaching out, his life might have been a series of rejections and depression. But he didn't let his handicap stand in the way of his creativity. And my life too felt transformed at that special moment.

When we create from what is most vital in us, our lives feel represented, our creations have meaning. And we learn and grow in the process. Silvano Arieti wrote, "Although creativity is by no means the only way in which the human being can grow, it is one of the most important. The growth occurs not only in the creative person but in all those who are affected by the innovation . . . art, literature, and music are essential to achieve a spiritual level of life in which discord and hate are less likely to occur."[18] The same is true, I may add, for any form of creativity. Just remember John.

Here are some further tips to keep yourself in the creative mode. Remember that:

> Creativity is a state of mind; it can transform the ordinary into the extraordinary.

Creativity requires *doing*, not just thinking about it.

Use *all* your feelings, the painful ones as well as the joyful ones.

Focus on what you *want*, rather than on what you don't want. For example, if you want to write, you'll have a much greater chance of doing so if you imagine yourself writing, rather than just saying to yourself: "If only I could write like Virginia Woolf."

Creative insights occur most frequently when you are off-guard and least expecting them. "Sleep on it," if you wish.

And do remember to play.

The journey does not end here. You have the power to begin it again and again.

Notes

1. Rollo May, *The Courage to Create* (New York: Bantam Books, 1976), 46.
2. Jeanne Segal, *Living Beyond Fear* (Hollywood: Newcastle Publishing Co., 1984).
3. Clement Russo, "Laughter: A Creative Muse?" *Psychology Today* (September 1987): 21.
4. Phyllis Greenacre, *Emotional Growth: Psychoanalytic Studies of the Gifted and a Great Variety of Other Individuals*, vol. 1 (New York: International Universities Press, 1971): 360–61.
5. Daniel Goleman, "Humor Found to Aid Problem-Solving." *The New York Times*, August 4, 1987, pp. C1, C8.
6. Sigmund Freud, in James Strachey, ed., *Standard Edition of the Complete Psychological Works of Sigmund Freud*, vol. 26 (London: Hogarth Press, 1963), 375–77.
7. Silvano Arieti, *Creativity: The Magic Synthesis* (New York: Basic Books, 1976), 30–31.
8. Ibid., 281.

9. Freud, in James Strachey, ed., *Standard Edition of the Complete Psychological Works of Sigmund Freud*, vol. 26, 375–77.

10. Alice Miller, (Switzerland) "Depression and Grandiosity as Related Forms of Narcissistic Disturbances." *The International Review of Psychoanalysis*, 6 (1979): 61–76.

11. Ira Progoff, *Waking Dream and Living Myth in the Creative Work of Ingmar Bergman* (Dialogue House Library Tape, 1979).

12. Stanley Krippner, "Into the Mythic Underground." *Association for Humanistic Psychology Newsletter* (April 1982): 1.

13. Carl Jung, the famous Swiss psychologist, emphasized that by discovering the unconscious anima (female) that lies within every male and unconscious animus (male) that lies within every female, the person is better able to resolve difficulties with the opposite sex. In this case Ginny was depending too much on Jim for a strength that existed within her.

14. A lucid dream is one in which the dreamer knows he or she is dreaming.

15. Anaïs Nin, in Evelyn J. Hinz, ed., *A Woman Speaks: The Lectures, Seminars, and Interviews of Anaïs Nin*. (Chicago: The Swallow Press, 1975), 122.

16. Joseph M. Winski, "Solidly Ensconced, Lear Builds Franchise." *Advertising Age* (October 23, 1989).

17. Sharon Begly, "The Stuff that Dreams are Made of." *Newsweek* (August 14, 1989): 41–47.

18. Arieti, *Creativity: The Magic Synthesis*, 413.

Bibliography

Ames, Barbara Edwards. "Dreams and Painting: A Case Study of the Relationship Between an Artist's Dreams and Painting." Ed.D. diss., University of Virginia, 1978.

Arieti, Silvano. *Creativity: The Magic Synthesis.* New York: Basic Books, 1976.

Barrios, Michael V., and Jerome L. Singer. "The Treatment of Creative Blocks: A Comparison of Waking Imagery, Hypnotic Dream, and Rational Discussion Techniques." *Imagination, Cognition and Personality.* 1 (1981–82): 89–109.

Barron, Frank. "Head and Heart Together." *AHP Perspective.* (June 1986): 12–13.

Begley, Sharon. "The Stuff that Dreams are Made of." *Newsweek* (August 14, 1989): 41–47.

Boettger, Suzaan. "Regression in the Service of . . ." *Art Criticism.* 2 (1986): 58–64.

Boice, Robert. "Contingency Management in Writing and the Appearance of Creative Ideas: Implications for the Treatment of Writing Blocks." *Behavior Research and Therapy* 21 (1983): 537–43.

Briggs, John. "Unshrouding the Muse: The Anatomy of Inspiration." *Art News* (April 1980): 52–55.

Broad, William J. "Tracing the Skeins of Matter." *The New York Times Magazine* (May 6, 1984): 54–62.

Durio, Helen F. "Mental Imagery and Creativity." *The Journal of Creative Behavior* 9 (1975): 233–44.

Edel, Leon. *Stuff of Sleep and Dreams: Experiments in Literary Psychology.* New York: Harper & Row, 1982.

Ehrenzweig, Anton. *The Hidden Order of Art.* Berkeley: University of California Press, 1967.

Field, Joanna. *On Not Being Able to Paint.* Los Angeles: J.P. Tarcher, 1957.

Fitzgerald, M. "Certain Vagaries: Robert Smithson, Science, and Surrealism." *Arts Magazine* 57 (May 1983): 126–28.

Freud, Sigmund. *On Creativity and the Unconscious.* New York: Harper & Row, 1958.

Freud, Sigmund. In James Strachey, ed. *Standard Edition of the Complete Psychological Works of Sigmund Freud.* London: Hogarth Press, Vol 1: 256 (1897); Vol 2: 207, 218 (1894); Vol 9: 7–9, 41–2, 46, 54, 62, 91–92, 94, 142–5 (1916); Vol 16: 375–7 (1917); Vol 23: 32, 41, 70–2, 87, 136, 149, 191 (1938); 286 (1940).

Fromm, Erich. "The Creative Attitude." In Harold H. Anderson, ed. *Creativity and Cultivation.* New York: Harper & Row, 1959.

Garai, Josef E. "New Horizons of the Humanistic Approach to Expressive Therapies and Creativity Development." *Art Psychotherapy* 6 (1979): 177–84.

Gardner, Howard. "Science Grapples With the Creative Puzzle." *The New York Times* May 13, 1984, pp. 1, 28.

Gedo, John E. *Portraits of the Artist.* New York: Guilford Press, 1983.

Ghiselin, Brewster, ed. *The Creative Process.* Berkeley: University of California Press, 1954.

Glynn, Eugene David. "The Deepest Necessity: Art and Creativity in Recent Psychoanalytic Theory." *Print Collector's Newsletter* 8 (May–June 1977): 29–35.

Goldstein, Virginia Barclay. "A Way to Creativity." *New Realities* 5 (1984): 38–42.

Goleman, Daniel. "A New Index Illuminates The Creative Life." *The New York Times.* September 13, 1988, pp. C1, C9.

Goleman, Daniel. "New View of Mind Gives Unconscious an Expanded Role." *The New York Times.* February 7, 1984, pp. C1, C2.

Goleman, Daniel. "Personal Myths Bring Cohesion to the Chaos of Each Life." *The New York Times.* May 24, 1988, pp. C1, C11.

Gordon, William J., and Tony Poze. "Conscious/Subconscious Interaction in a Creative Act." *Journal of Creative Behavior.* 15 (1981): 1–10.

Gotz, Ignacio L. "On Defining Creativity." *The Journal of Aesthetics and Art Criticism* 39 (Spring 1981) 297–301.

Greenacre, Phyllis. *Emotional Growth: Psychoanalytic Studies of the Gifted and a Great Variety of Other Individuals.* New York: International Universities Press, Inc. 1971.

———. *The Quest for the Father.* New York: International Universities Press, 1963.

Hedlund, Dalva E., Tanis C. Furst, and Kathryn T. Foley. "A Dialogue with Self: The Journal as an Educational Tool." *Journal of Humanistic Education and Development* 27 (1989): 105–13.

Henning, Lawrence H. "Paradox as a Treatment For Writer's Block." *Personnel and Guidance Journal* 60 (October 1981): 112–13.

Hofstadter, Douglas R. "Metamagical Themas." *Scientific American* (October 1982): 20–28.

Holden, Constance. "Creativity and the Troubled Mind." *Psychology Today* (April 1987): 9, 10.

Hospers, John. "Artistic Creativity." *The Journal of Aesthetics and Art Criticism* 43 (Spring 1985): 43–55.

Houston, Jean. "The Psychenaut Program: An Exploration into Some Human Potentials." *The Journal of Creative Behavior.* 7 (1973): 253–78.

Hulse-Stephens, David. "Writers on Writing." *New Dimensions* (March–April 1989): 6, 7.

Hunt, Morton. "How the Mind Works." *The New York Times Magazine* (January 24, 1982): 30–33.

Jones, A.C. "Grandiosity Blocks Writing Projects." *Transactional Analysis Journal* 5 (1975): 415.

Jung, C.G. "The Relations Between Ego and the Unconscious." In *The Basic Writings of C.G. Jung.* New York: Random House, 1959.

Kohn, Alfie. "Art for Art's Sake." *Psychology Today* (September 1987): 52–57.

Krippner, Stanley. "Access to Hidden Reserves of the Unconscious Through Dreams in Creative Problem Solving." *The Journal of Creative Behavior* 15 (1981): 11–22.

————. "Into the Mythic Underground." *Association for Humanistic Psychology Newsletter* (April 1982): 1.

Krippner, Stanley and Joseph Dillard. *Dreamworking*. Buffalo, New York: Bearly Limited, 1987.

Kronsky, Betty J. "Freeing the Creative Process: The Relevance of Gestalt." *Art Psychotherapy* 6 (1979): 233–40.

Kubie, Lawrence S. *Neurotic Distortion of the Creative Process*. New York: Noonday Press, 1958.

Lamberg, Lynne. "Night Pilot." *Psychology Today* (July–August 1988): 35–42.

Lambert, Don. "Reflections of a Genius." *Saturday Review* (January–February 1984): 22–25.

Langer, Cassandra. "The Art of Healing." *Ms* (January–February 1989): 132–33.

Leo, John. Reported by William Blaylock. "The Ups and Downs of Creativity." *Time*. (October 8, 1984): p. 76.

Lerner, Leila. "Discussion of Imagery and the Self in Artistic Creativity and Psychoanalytic Literary Criticism." *The Psychoanalytic Review*, 68 (Fall 1981): 421–24.

MacLeod, Gordon A. "Does Creativity Lead to Happiness and More Enjoyment in Life?" *The Journal of Creative Behavior* 7 (1973): 227–30.

Mandell, Johnathan. "Talking the Mystery Out of Dreams." *Newsday* (February 2, 1988): 4, 5.

May, Rollo. *The Courage to Create*. New York: Bantam Books, 1975.

McAleer, Neil. "On Creativity." *Omni* (April 1989).

McCully, Robert S. "Archetypal Energy and the Creative Image." *The Journal of Analytic Psychology* 21 (January 1976): 64–71.

McNiff, Shaun. "On Art Therapy: A Conversation with Rudolf Arnheim." *Art Psychotherapy* 2 (1975): 195–202.

Mednick, S. "The Associative Basis of the Creative Process." *Psychological Review* 69 (1962): 221.

Miller, Alice (Switzerland). "Depression and Grandiosity As Related Forms of Narcissistic Disturbances." *The International Review of Psychoanalysis*. (Vol 6) 1979: 61–76.

Momigliano, Luciana Nissim (Milan). "From an Analyst's Notebook: Some Considerations on Writing a Paper." *The International Review of Psycho-Analysis* 9, (1982): 45–54.

Munro, T. "The Psychology of Art: Past, Present, Future." In James Hogg, ed. *Psychology and the Visual Arts*. Baltimore: Penguin Books, 1969.

Musick, Patricia L. "Creative Emergence: A Synthesis." *Art Psychotherapy* 6 (1979): 213–19.

Noy, Pinchas. "A Revision of the Psychoanalytic Theory of the Primary Process." *The International Journal of Psycho-Analysis* 50 (1969): 155–78.

O'Toole, Patricia. "Creative Thinking: Can Imagination Be Learned?" *Vogue* (December 1983): 148, 153.

Policoff, Stephen Phillip. "In Search of the Elusive Aha!" *New Age Journal* (March 1985): 43–49.

Rank, Otto. *The Courage to Create.* New York: Bantam Books, 1975.

Raudsepp, Eugene. "Profile of the Creative Individual," part 1. *Creative Computing* (August 1983): 170–209.

Rhodes, Richard. "You Can Direct Your Dreams." *Parade Magazine* (February 19, 1984): 10,11.

Robbins, Lois B. *Waking up in the Age of Creativity.* Santa Fe, N.M.: Bear & Company, 1985.

Rodgers, Carl. "Toward a Theory of Creativity." In *On Becoming A Person.* Boston: Houghton Mifflin, 1961.

Roland, Alan. "Imagery and the Self in Artistic Creativity and Psychoanalytic Literary Criticism." *The Psychoanalytic Review* 68 (Fall 1981): 409–20.

Rosen, Mickie. "The Effects of the Psychotherapeutic Process Upon the Creative Process." *Art Psychotherapy* 2 (1975): 137–47.

Rosica, James Amedeo. *Creativity: An Examination, Analysis and Synthesis of Conscious and Unconscious Theories.* Ed.D. diss., Rutgers University–The State University of New Jersey (New Brunswick), 1982.

Sachs, Hanns. *The Creative Unconscious: Studies in the Psychoanalysis of Art.* (edited by A.A. Roback). Cambridge, Massachusetts: Sci-Art Publishers, 1951.

Sang, Barbara E. "Women and the Creative Process." *The Arts in Psychotherapy* 8 (1981): 43–48.

Segal, William. "Sleep and the Inner Landscape." In *Leaning On The Moment.* New York: Parabola Books, 1986: 55–68.

States, Bert O. *The Rhetoric of Dreams.* New York: Cornell University Press, 1989.

Storr, Anthony. *The Dynamics of Creation.* New York: Atheneum, 1985.

Taft, Ronald. "Creativity: Hot and Cold." *Journal of Personality* 39 (September 1971): 345–61.

Ullman, Montague, ed., and Claire Limmer. *The Variety of Dream Experience.* New York: Continuum, 1987.

Von Franz, Marie-Louise, filmed conversation with Fraser Boa. *The Way of the Dream*. Toronto: Windrose Films Ltd., 1988.

Walker, Alan. "Music and the Unconscious." *British Medical Journal* 2 (December 15, 1979): 1641–43.

Wallace, Edith. "For C.G. Jung's One Hundredth Birthday: Creativity and Jungian Thought." *Art Psychotherapy* 2 (1975): 181–87.

Wallace, William H. "Some Dimensions of Creativity. Part 2." *Personnel Journal* 46 (1967): 438–43.

Wayne, June. "The Creative Process: Artists, Carpenters, and the Flat Earth Society." *Craft Horizons* 36 (October 1976): 30, 31.

Weininger, O. "Play, Creativity and the Cognitive Unconscious." *Reading Improvement* 18 (Summer 1981): 98–107.

Wilson, Robert Anton. "Colin Wilson." *New Age Journal* (April 1985): 59–66.

Winnicott, D.W. *Playing and Reality*. New York: Basic Books, 1971.

Young, John G. "What is Creativity?" *The Journal of Creative Behavior* 19 (1987): 77–87.

Zdenek, Marilee. *The Right-Brain Experience*. New York: McGraw-Hill, 1983.

Index

259